DICK WE

attitudes

2

"He Sent Forth His Word and Healed Them" PSALMS 107:20

Virgil Leach

QUALITY PUBLICATIONS

P.O. BOX 1060   ABILENE, TEXAS 79604

1. God is the source that all that live.

2. Of him + thru him in all things
   God is self existant

3. God is eternal — Deut 30:27 Psm 9:
   Jer 16:18
   LAM 5:19
   1 Tim 1:1

4. God is good

5. God is strong because he is infin
   1. Omnipresent
   2. Infinate in his knowledge — Omn

6. God is immutable — cannot d

MICAH

FOREWORD

It is fortunate when one has talent, but talent is cheap. You can buy it, people sell it; you can find it everywhere. But attitudes are not for sale. You can't buy an attitude for a million dollars. We are literally surrounded by talent. We see it in school, in business, in government, even in our own homes. Again it is everywhere! But we are also aware that there are millions of talented alcoholics. There is no way to compare talents with attitudes.

Not only is talent cheap, so is education. You can get it. It is available everywhere. Most anyone can receive a degree or even a whole string of them if he wants to. But let us remember there are millions of educated derelicts. There is no way to compare education with attitudes.

Also we find all around us an abundance of aptitude. It is also cheap. But again attitudes are just not for sale. How wonderful it would be if every teacher would pass on attitudes as the one great thing to be gained for our young people.

It is not so much what a person knows or is able to do or possess but rather the question is what kind of person am I. Perhaps all of us have witnessed only too often an ugly spirit or attitude that has brought great harm. A bad attitude can spoil almost any situation. On the other hand, a good attitude can enhance, or make right almost any adverse condition that may exist.

The Value Of This Manual

Just ask mothers and fathers all over our country; they will tell you what their children need. They will immediately affirm that this material is vital, needed, and gets specifically to the point. Question every employer, school-teacher, elder, judge, statesman or those from a broken home; in every case they will reply the same. This book contains a simple, sincere, understandable code for training youth that will prepare them for the future that lies so precariously before them. It will have its effect on them in a positive way and be of eternal worth.

Careful and skillful hands have gathered the best possible material. Its practical value rests on the fact that it may be used in the church, the home, and in connection with any of the plans you may have for the development of your young people.

Training youths is our most important responsibility. It should come before all else. This manual presents a new and refreshing approach to getting the job done. The lessons are superior and will guard against the pitfalls of life. Each lesson gets to the heart and soul of developing Christian characteristics, and presents standards we've always hoped to achieve in our sons and daughters. It gives complete analysis of attitudes vital to every living person and how to develop them. We must remember that our number one problem everywhere is attitude.

The commentary, the Scripture back-up, questions and assignments leave an unforgettable impression, and will bless the student and teacher alike. It will be a pleasure to teach. Our whole aim is to fashion lives into the image and likeness of the Savior who grew in wisdom and stature, and in favor with God and man. Each lesson is in touch with life's realities, deals with daily needs and will become a bulwark of strength to enable them to be all they should be in the home, school, marriage, church or whatever vocation they might choose in life.

Perhaps in the past we have been too vague and general in presenting the ideals of proper attitudes, responsibility and Christian character. We believe that it would be well for every teacher, regardless of what age group being taught, to have this material in their hands, even if used no more than a supplement to their class. Let it be at their finger-tips as a constant companion, counselor and co-worker. It will equip them to see more clearly what the real aim of their class should be, and will be a gage to spiritual maturity.

ATTITUDES 2 includes 26 valuable attitude lessons, enough for a six-month course of study. **ATTITUDES 1** is also available for 26 more lessons on attitudes.

This entire book is designed for Teacher's Manuals. Should Student Workbook be desired, use only exercises with blanks and fill-in-Scriptures plus the suggested assignments. Use Revised Standard Version except where King James Version is specificed.

TABLE OF CONTENTS

Attitude Game Board

Attitude games have many options; of course, it is wise first to have several lessons on attitudes before using attitude games. The game not only provides an interesting and exciting diversion but also makes learning fun.

One may use attitude games in learning centers to test how much students have grasp or retained from the teachers lessons. At the same time it provides a technique of learning how to apply scripture and interpret them in their true light. This is an urgent need.

Contests can be had between as few as 2 students or as many as 30 depending on the occasion or size of the class. For example all the boys may compete with all the girls. This can be done when the teacher reads a particular scripture holding it up before the class. The teacher then asks for a show of hands to see who knows where the scripture applies and to what particular attitude. The teacher alternates between boys and girls. Each side takes their respective turn to answer. The side that gets the most correct - wins.

When only two or four compete with each other, then all scriptures must be placed in a container. Each contestant in turn reaches into the container to draw out one scripture at a time which he places on proper square of the attitude board. Use a watch or a three minute sand glass to see who can place the most scriptures on proper setting in the least amount of time.

Another option: the instructor can use the board as a review for students. Give each student a sheet of paper and have him write down the proper attitudes as teacher reads the scripture.

This board is made of wood and the scriptures are placed on the removable circular rings. These rings have small punched out holes which enable them to be fastened to the nails on the board.

Attitude Boards can be made with less expense and work by using poster board for both the rings and board.

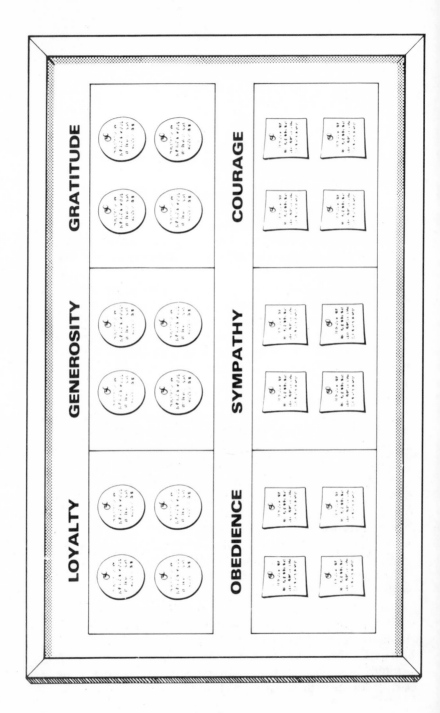

8

ATTITUDES
TEACHER'S CHECK LIST

LOYALTY

Philippians 3:8
Philippians 2:30
Matthew 16:24
Acts 21:13

OBEDIENCE

Hebrews 10:26
Matthew 7:21
Poverbs 1:24
Ephesians 6:2-3

TEMPER

Ephesians 4:26
Ecclesiastes 7:9
Matthew 5:22
I John 2:11

GENEROSITY

John 3:16
Acts 20:35
Luke 19:8
II Corinthians 9:7

SYMPATHY

Proverbs 21:13
Romans 12:15
I Corinthians 12:26
Hebrews 4:5

COURAGE

Philippians 4:13
Isaiah 40:29
Joshua 1:5-6
Numbers 13:33

GRATITUDE

I Timothy 4:4
Psalms 150:6
Romans 1:21
Malachi 2:2

MORALITY

Romans 1:24
Hebrews 13:4
Galatians 5:19
II Timothy 2:22

GOOD SPEECH

I Peter 3:10
Matthew 12:36
Proverbs 17:7
Proverbs 18:21

TRUTHFULNESS

Proverbs 19:9
Proverbs 6:16
Psalms 101:7
Acts 5:3

KINDNESS

Romans 12:20
Ephesians 4:32
Matthew 5:44
Luke 6:35

AMBITION

Proverbs 18:9
II Chronicles 31:21
II Thess. 3:10
I Corinthians 15:58

9

AIM HIGH

"Make no little plans: They have no magic to stir men's blood and probably themselves will not be realized. Make big plans: Aim high in hope and work, remembering that a noble, logical diagram once recorded will never die, but long after we are gone will be a living thing; asserting itself with ever growing insistency. Remember that our sons and grandsons are going to do things that would stagger us."

—Daniel Burnham

Responsibility

Paul, the apostle to the Gentiles, wrote to the Romans, "For Macedonia and Achaia have been pleased to make some contribution for the poor among the saints at Jerusalem; they were pleased to do it, and indeed they are in debt to them, for if the Gentiles have come to share in their spiritual blessings, they ought also to be of service to them in material blessings" (Romans 15:26, 27).

Responsibility is the state of being answerable or accountable, as for an obligation either moral or legal.

The lesson of responsibility is one of the most difficult to learn, since the idea of our being free is a deeply rooted conviction and we are prone to resent my restraints whatever upon our freedom. Nevertheless, that person is handicapped in the race for success who was not taught early in life to be responsible for something worthwhile. Not only does responsibility develop character, but the world would be in utter chaos if there were not those willing and able to accept responsibility and perform according to its dictates.

Henry Ward Beecher said, "All higher motives, ideals, conceptions, sentiments in a man are of no account if they do not come forward to strengthen him for the better discharge of the duties which devolve upon him in the ordinary affairs of life."

When we come to realize that freedom merely means that we are not owned by another human, but that each and every one of us is obligated to our fellow man to perform certain functions for the good of mankind in general, as well as for our own benefit, then, and only then, will we have made any progress in the development of this necessary virtue.

Let us take inventory, so to speak, of our responsibilities and see that we fulfill them each day. If we would really grow, we might look

11

about us and see if there are not other tasks which we might perform that have not yet been required of us. This would not only relieve someone else who is now having to shoulder responsibilities that we could help meet - someone of our associates, probably our parents or another member of our family - but it would be a most effective step in our preparation for a successful life.

Fill in Scriptures

1. _____ Here am I send me.

2. _____ If any one does not provide for his relatives and especially for his own family, he has disowned the faith and is worse than an unbeliever.

3. _____ I am debtor (under obligation) both to Greeks and to barbarians, both to the wise and to the foolish: so I am eager to preach . . . .

4. _____ It is required of stewards that they be found trustworthy.

5. _____ Be stedfast, immovable, always abounding in the work of the Lord.

6. _15-4_ Woe to me if I do not preach . . . . *I Cor*

7. _____ If you warn the wicked to turn from his way . . . you will have saved your life.

8. _____ Let your light so shine before men . . .

9. _____ Bear one another's burdens.

10. _____ Go into all the world and preach the gospel.

11. _____ Admonish the idle, encourage the faint-hearted, help the weak.

12. _22:5_ They made light of it. *Matt*

13. _____ By this time you ought to be teachers.

14. _____ They all alike began to make excuses.

15. _____ Whatever you wish that men would do to you, do so to them.

16. _____ What does it profit, . . . if a man says he has faith but has not works?

17. _____ We must obey God rather than men.

Acts 5:29	Luke 14:18	Ezekiel 33:9
Isaiah 6:8	1 Corinthians 9:16	1 Thessalonians 5:14
James 2:14	Hebrews 5:12	Matthew 5:16
1 Timothy 5:8	1 Corinthians 4:2	Galatians 6:2
Matthew 7:12	Matthew 22:5	Mark 16:15
Romans 1:14, 15	1 Corinthians 15:58	

Questions for Discussion

1. Define responsibility.

2. Do you feel that this is one of your strong characteristics?

3. Could you wish to be closely associated with those who avoid, shift or shirk responsibility?

4. What should be the basic responsibilities of life?

5. What is excuse-making?

6. In your church, who is responsible to visit the sick, teach Bible classes, give liberally, seek the lost, attend all the assemblies, be friendly to visitors and pray without ceasing?

7. Where have you shown responsibility in building the church?

8. Why do some have a light and trivial attitude toward God-given responsibility?

9. Is it right to say that one who is slack in his work is a brother to a destroyer?

10. Is the "sin of doing nothing" a real problem in the church?

11. Could it be said that one of life's greatest achievements is to become reliable and fully responsible in sharing worthy church activities?

12. Summarize the need, blessings and rewards of being responsible.

STATEMENT: Gifford Pinchot said, "There is no more valuable subordinate than the man to whom you can give a piece of work and then forget it, in the confident expectation that the next time it is brought to your attention it will come in the form of a report that the thing has been done."

Suggested Assignments:

1. Memorize Romans 12:12; 1 Corinthians 4:1, 2.

2. Construct sentences of the following words: responsibility, lazy, accountable, work, reliable, negligent, untrustworthy.

Titus 3- 8, to 14

3. Visit a convalescent home for the aged or shut-in.

4. Volunteer to do some task about the home that is not normally required; vacuum floors; clean out garage, etc.

5. Write a note of appreciation to some worthy person.

Sincerity

Writing to Titus, Paul said, "In all things shewing thyself a pattern of good works: in doctrine shewing uncorruptness, gravity, sincerity, sound speech that cannot be condemned; that he that is of the contrary part may be ashamed, having no evil thing to say of you" (Titus 2:7, 8 KJV).

Sincerity is the state or quality of being true or genuine; honesty; straight-forwardness; uprightness.

It is a quality that is greatly to be desired, and one that cannot be overstressed. Sincerity means that we do not make a pretense of being something which we are not, and is the opposite of hypocrisy. God's Word teaches us to "put away all malice and all guile and insincerity and envy and all slander" (1 Peter 2:1). And again we read, "The wisdom from above is first pure, then peaceable, gentle, open to reason, full of mercy and good fruits, without uncertainty or insincerity" (James 3:17).

Many times Jesus spoke scathingly against the hypocrisy of those religious leaders who set themselves up as examples of piety, yet refused to obey God. We may be sure that we, too, will be condemned if we do not act and speak sincerely at all times.

Even the world despises hypocrisy. Those who practice it, thinking it easier than changing themselves to be that which they admire and wish others to think them to be, receive very little respect. Not many people are fooled by it, in the first place, but even if we could make everyone believe that we are something which we are not, God knows what we are and will judge us accordingly.

Paul wrote, "And this I pray, that your love may abound yet more and more in knowledge and in all my judgment; that ye may approve things that are excellent; that ye may be sincere and without offence till the day of Christ'' (Philippians 1:9, 10 KJV). These passages, though only a few of the many that exhort us to be sincere, are enough to convince us that it is God's will that we practice sincerity at all times.

Fill in Scriptures

1. *[handwritten: I Cor. 2, 17]* We are not, like so many, peddlers of God's word; but as men of sincerity, as commissioned of God.

2. *[handwritten: II Cor. 1, 12]* Our boast is this, the testimony of our conscience that we have behaved in the world, and still more toward you, with holiness and godly sincerity.

3. *[handwritten: Josh. 24:14]* Now therefore, fear the Lord, and serve him in sincerity and in faithfulness.

4. *[handwritten: Gal. 2, 11, 13]* Cephas. . .stood condemned. . .he drew back and separated himself, fearing the circumcision party. And with him the rest of the Jews acted insincerely, so that even Barnabas was carried away by their insincerity.

5. *[handwritten: Matt 15, 8]* This people honors me with their lips, but their heart is far from me; in vain do they worship me.

6. *[handwritten: Judg. 9, 19]* If you then have acted in good faith and honor. . .then rejoice.

7. *[handwritten: Matt 23, 5]* They do all their deeds to be seen of men.

8. *[handwritten: II Cor. 8, 8]* I say this not as a command, but to prove by the earnestness of others that your love also is genuine.

9. *[handwritten: Matt 23, 27]* Woe to you scribes and Pharisees, hypocrites! for you are like whitewashed tombs, which outwardly appear beautiful, but within they are full of dead men's bones and all uncleanness.

10. *[handwritten: Lk. 16, 15]* You are those who justify yourselves before men, but God knows your hearts.

11. *[handwritten: I Tim. 4, 1]* Some will depart from the faith by giving heed to deceitful spirits, and doctrines of demons, through the pretensions of liars whose conscience are seared.

12. *[handwritten: Prov. 20:17]* Bread gained by deceit is sweet to a man, but afterwards his mouth will be full of gravel.

Proverbs 20:17   2 Corinthians 2:17   2 Corinthians 1:12
Joshua 24:14   2 Corinthians 8:8   Galatians 2:11-13
Matthew 15:8, 9   Judges 9:19   Matthew 23:5
Matthew 23:27   Luke 16:15   1 Timothy 4:1, 2

Questions for Discussion

1. Define sincerity.

2. Why is insincerity so replusive to both the church and the world?

3. When is one most likely to be tempted into pretense, deception or cheating?

4. Why may some desire to appear well before men without paying the price of what being right costs?

5. Define a hypocrite.

6. What may one hope to gain by being hypocritical?

7. There are two kinds of hypocrisy; one is where men pretend to be better than they really are, and the other is where men pretend to be worse than they are—that is, they fail to witness for Christ for fear of ridicule or rejection. In your judgment which is the worst sin?

8. Can neutrality and silence be a cover-up for one's insincerity?

9. How does insincerity affect the conscience?

10. How do you feel personally toward those who cheat, mislead others, or deliberately cover up the truth?

11. Should we not hate every false way?

12. Summarize the need, blessings and rewards of sincerity.

Suggested Assignments

1. Memorize Matthew 15:8, 9; 2 Corinthians 2:17.

2. Make sentences of the following words: pretense, hypocrite, honesty, deceit, sincerity.

Interest

The apostle Paul, writing to the Philippians regarding sending Timothy to them, said, "I have no one like him, who will be genuinely anxious for your welfare. They all look after their own interests, not those of Jesus Christ" (Philippians 2:20, 21).

Interest is defined as the tendency to give attention to an object, situation, or idea; to cause to take a share in; to produce an effect upon.

Attention and interest are closely allied. It is natural that each of us should have an interest in things; even a baby will show an interest in light, sound, and the like at a very early age. The important thing is that we train ourselves to focus our interest upon things worthy of attention; things which will build us up for a good life here, and prepare us for eternal life.

Many people, both children and adults, have never cultivated any real interests, but have been in the habit of focusing their attention upon whatever appealed to their fancy for the moment. Such persons can never achieve success, nor can they know contentment, for without our interests we are bored and restless. We should strive to make our lives full and happy with worthwhile interest.

The apostle Paul knew that Timothy would have a real interest and concern for the spiritual welfare of the Philippians because he was deeply interested in Christ and His kingdom. His life was dedicated to Christian works. No one can have a greater interest than this!

Paul was made happy because the Philippians were interested in sharing his work for the Lord. We read in Philippians 4:10-17, "I rejoice in the Lord greatly that now at length you have revived your concern for me; you were indeed concerned for me, but you had no opportunity. Not that I complain of want; for I have learned, in whatever state I am, to be content. . . Yet it was kind of you to share my trouble. And you Philippians yourselves know that in the beginning of the gospel, when I left Macedonia, no church entered into partnership with me in giving and receiving except you only; for even in Thessalonica you sent me help once and again. Not that I seek the gift; but I seek the fruit which increases to your credit.''

Each of us should cultivate an interest in the spread of the gospel. If we are unable to take it to others ourselves, we can have an interest in this work by helping those Christians who can go in person. This will be, as Paul told the Philippians, ''fruit which will increase to (our) credit.''

Fill in Scriptures

1. _____ Seek the things that are above, where Christ is seated. . . Set your minds on things above, not on things that are on earth.

2. _____ I have no one like him, who will be genuinely anxious for your welfare. They all look after their own interests, not those of Jesus Christ.

3. _____ Whoever seeks to gain his life will lose it, but whoever loses his life will preserve it.

4. _____ ''I will do this; I will pull down my barns, and build larger ones; and there I will store all my grain and my goods. And I will say to my soul, Soul, you have ample goods laid up for many years; take your ease, eat, drink, be merry.'' But God said to him, ''Fool!''

5. _____ To those who by patience in well-doing seek for glory and honor and immortality, he will give eternal life.

6. _____ My heart's desire and prayer to God for them is that they may be saved.

7. _____ As for what was sown among thorns, this is he who hears the word, but the cares of the word and delight in riches choke the word, and it proves unfruitful.

8. _____ Indeed I count everything as loss because of the surpassing worth of knowing Christ Jesus my Lord.

For his sake I have suffered the loss of all things, and count them as refuse, in order that I may gain Christ.

9._____Martha, Martha, you are anxious and troubled about many things; one thing is needful. Mary has chosen the good portion, which shall not be taken away from her.

10._____Therefore whoever wishes to be a friend of the world makes himself an enemy of God.

11._____I made me great works; I built houses and planted vineyards for myself; I made myself gardens and parks, and planted in them all kinds of fruit trees. I made myself pools. . . I bought male and female slaves, . . . I had also great possessions of herds and flocks. . . I also gathered for myself silver and gold and treasure. . . Behold, all was vanity and striving after wind.

Colossians 3:1-2
Luke 10:41
Romans 10:1
James 4:4

Luke 17:33
Philippians 2:20-21
Philippians 3:8
Ecclesiastes 2:4-11

Romans 2:7
Luke 12:18-20
Matthew 13:22

Questions for Discussion

1. Define interest.
2. What is the main difference between natural interest and acquired interest?
3. Name several natural predominate interests among men or women.
4. Name the basic acquired interests that men or women must develop.
5. How do natural interest and acquired interest compare in value?
6. How did Jesus get people's attention?
7. What is the difference between attention and interest?
8. What does one do to develop acquired interest?
9. What do we mean by divided interest?
10. Is it wrong to have natural interest?
11. What are some obstacles one must face in placing acquired

interest over natural interest?

12. Summarize the need, blessing and rewards of developing acquired interests.

Suggested Assignments

1. Memorize Philippians 3:7, 8.

2. Make a list of your main natural interest and your acquired interest.

3. Make sentences of the following words: attention; natural interest; acquired interest.

Reverence

We read in Hebrews 12:28, "Therefore let us be grateful for receiving a kingdom that cannot be shaken, and thus let us offer to God acceptable worship, with reverence and awe."

Reverence is deep respect together with awe and affection; veneration; honor; homage; deference; to hold in high regard or esteem.

Reverence is closely akin to respect, except that it goes further, being profound respect mingled with both affection and fear. The command, "Fear God," does not mean to be afraid of Him, but to respect Him deeply and with a large measure of love and veneration. It is impossible to reverence anything common; lesser objects are given lesser emotions.

Both respect and reverence are attitudes of the heart and cannot be called forth merely upon demand. As we think of God and learn of His love for us, our thoughts and feelings become respectful because of what He is and represents, and they become reverent because of His character and relationship to us. Thus, we see that our reverence for God is dependent upon our realization of Him as our creator and eternal savior.

Jesus, speaking to the Jews who sought to kill him, said: ". . . you refuse to come to me that you may have life. I do not receive glory from men. But I know that you have not the love of God within you" (John 5:40-42). And the apostle John wrote, "By this we may be sure that we know him, if we keep his commandments. He who says 'I know him' but disobeys his commandments is a liar, and the truth is not in him; but whoever keeps his word, in him truly love for God is perfected. By this we may be sure that

24

we are in him: he who says he abides in him ought to walk in the same way in which he walked" (1 John 2:3-6).

We see, then, that to show love and reverence for God we must obey His Word, and He has promised to give us eternal life in return. Let us carefully and prayerfully study His Word, obey His commands, and with reverence in our hearts worship Him in spirit and in truth.

"Great and wonderful are thy deeds O Lord God the Almighty! Just and true are thy ways, O King of the ages! Who shall not fear and glorify thy name, O Lord? For thou alone art holy" (Revelation 15:3-4 RSV).

Perhaps most of us could cultivate a greater depth of feeling of awe and majesty. Let us acknowledge Him in all our ways. He is omnipotent, omniscient and omnipresent. We must recognize Him as the sustainer of our very lives and "the giver of every good and perfect gift." Think of Him as your Creator, Father, Friend and Judge. Think of Him as the one who has said, "I have graven you on the palms of my hands" (Isaiah 49:16 RSV). Love Him! Honor Him! Obey Him! Worship Him! Let your reverence be felt and let it be known. Don't let others guess of your reverence for Him.

"Praise the Lord, O my soul! I will praise the Lord as long as I live" (Psalms 146:1-2 RSV). "Let everything that breathes praise the Lord" (Psalms 150:6 RSV).

Fill in Scriptures

1. _Jhn 4:24_ God is spirit, and those who worship him must worship in spirit and truth.

2. _Hab 2:21_ But the Lord is in his holy temple; let all the earth keep silence before him.

3. _Ex 3:5_ Do not come near; put off your shoes from your feet, for the place on which you are standing is holy ground."

4. _____ Let everything that breathes praise the Lord!

5. _Rev. 6_ And from the throne came a voice crying, "Praise our God, all you his servants, you who fear him, small and great." Then I heard what seemed to be the voice of a great multitude . . . like the sound of mighty thunderpeals, crying "Hallelujah! For the Lord our God the Almighty reigns. . ."

6._____I will extol thee, my God and King, and bless thy name forever and ever and ever. Every day I will bless thee.

7._____Although they knew God they did not honor him as God or give thanks to him, but they became futile in their thinking and their senseless minds were darkened. Claiming to be wise, they became fools. . . .

8.*Matt 12:23* Immediately an angel of the Lord smote him, because he did not give God the glory; and he was eaten by worms and died.

9.___33:8 Let all the earth fear the Lord, let all the inhabitants of the world stand in awe of him!

10.*Mk 7:67* This people honors me with their lips, but their heart is far from me; in vain do they worship me, teaching as doctrine the precepts of men.

11._____I was glad when they said to me, "Let us go to the house of the Lord!"

12.*LK 17:18* Was no one found to return and give praise to God except this foreigner?

13.*Dan 4:25* You shall be driven from among men, and your dwelling shall be with the beasts of the field; you shall be made to eat grass like an ox, and you shall be wet with the dew of heaven . . . till you know that the Most High rules the kingdom of men. . . .

Psalms 145:1-2
Exodus 3:5
Psalms 33:8
Psalms 122:1
Revelation 19:5-6

Habakkuk 2:20
Daniel 4:25
Acts 12:23
John 4:24

Psalms 150:6
Mark 7:6-7
Luke 17:18
Romans 1:21-22

Questions for Discussion

1. Define reverence.

2. Can any part of worship be right or pleasing to God without reverence?

3. On what days of the week are we to show reverence to God?

4. How can one prepare himself properly for worship?

5. How does loud coughing, dropping song books, coming in late,

roving eyes, rattling papers, babies' prolonged crying, dull singing, also staying up for the late television shows on Saturday night, lack of Bible study, boredom, and non-involvement affect true worship?

6. When people say they don't get much out of worship, generally, whose fault is it?

7. Who is to be the main recipient of our worship—man or God?

8. How can we help one another to be more reverent?

9. Do we go to worship mainly to get something out of it or contribute to it?

10. Is reverence something that comes to a person naturally or must it be acquired?

11. Can you suggest something that could bring about a deeper relationship and communion with God?

12. What must take place first before there can be adoration and awe in the heart of the worshiper?

13. Summarize the need, blessings, and rewards of reverence.

Suggested Assignments

1. Memorize Psalms 145:1, 2; John 4:24.

2. Make sentences of the following words: worship, reverence, awe, honor, praise, veneration, adore.

3. Write a paragraph defining in some depth the real meaning of one of the four kinds of worship:

   A. True worship (John 4:24).
   B. Vain worship (Mark 7:7).
   C. Will worship (Colossians 2:22, 23).
   D. Ignorant worship (Acts 17:23).

Tenacity Of Purpose

Jesus, speaking to the man whom he had called, said, "No one who puts his hand to the plow and looks back is fit for the kingdom of God" (Luke 9:62).

Tenacity of purpose is defined as the state of quality of being able or inclined to hold fast to a purpose or aim.

"Stick-to-it-iveness," or tenacity of purpose, is the quality which enables us to finish every task begun. It enables us to do our duty completely, leaving no portion of our work unfinished. The people who succeed in life are the ones who, with a vise-like grip, take hold of life's problems and solve them. These are the ones who have done most to add to the progress and advancement of civilization. Such are the inventors, scientists, educators, to name but a few examples. The apostle Paul admonished the Thessalonians to "test everything; hold fast what is good, abstain from every form of evil" (1 Thessalonians 5:21).

We must not confuse tenacity of purpose with stubborness which usually, though not always, indicates unreasonable determination. **Remember, careful consideration should be given in establishing each aim or goal in our life. Having done this, let us hold fast to our purposes** and see them through to completion. We may be sure that we will meet with many obstacles and perhaps real hardships in our endeavor to reach our goals, and the higher the aim the more opposition we will have. Let us remember what James wrote to Christians, "Count it all joy, my brethren, when you meet various trials, for you know that the testing of your faith produces steadfastness. And let steadfastness have its full effect, that you may be perfect and complete, lacking in nothing" (James 1:2-4). And

27

Paul wrote, "Therefore, my beloved brethren, be steadfast, immovable, always abounding in the work of the Lord, knowing that in the Lord your labor is not in vain" (1 Corinthians 15:58). We can have no higher purpose than that of living a faithful, fruitful Christian life.

"There is no moment like the present. The man who will not execute his resolutions when they are fresh upon him can have no hope from them afterwards: they will be dissipated, lost, and perish in the hurry and scurry of the world, or sunk in the slough of indolence." These lines from the pen of Maria Edgeworth are all too true—there is no time like the present to begin to mold our lives in the image of Christ and become worthwhile Christians. He would have us be useful in this life to our associates and the world in general, then we will be better prepared for use in His kingdom.

Fill in Scriptures

1. _Acts 21:13_ Then Paul answered, "What are you doing, weeping and breaking my heart? For I am ready not only to be imprisoned but even die at Jerusalem for the name of the Lord Jesus"

2. _2 Thess 3:13_ Brethren, do not be weary in well-doing.

3. _____When the days drew near for him to be received up, he set his face to go to Jerusalem.

4. _____I can do all things in him who strengthens me.

5. _2 Tim 4:8_ I have fought the good fight, I have finished the race, I have kept the faith. Henceforth there is laid up for me a crown of righteousness.

6. _____In due season we shall reap, if we do not lose heart.

7. _____Therefore lift your drooping hands and strengthen your weak knees, and make straight paths for your feet.

8. _____Strive to enter by the narrow door; for many, I tell you, will seek to enter and will not be able.

9. _____If we have died with him, we shall also live with him, if we endure, we shall also reign with him . . . if we are faithless, he remains faithful—for he cannot deny himself.

10. _Acts 20:24_ But I do not account my life of any value nor as precious to myself, if only I may accomplish my course.

11. _Heb 2 0 12 4_ Let us hold fast the confession of our hope without wavering. . . . Let us consider how to stir up one another to love and good works.

12. _Gen 32:26_ I will not let you go unless you bless me.

13. _____ In these days he went out into the hills to pray; and all night he continued in prayer to God.

14. _matt 10:22_ He who endures to the end will be saved.

15. _____ They have not root in themselves, but endure for a while; then, when tribulation or persecution arises . . . they fall away.

Luke 9:51
2 Timothy 2:11-13
✓2 Thessalonians 3:13
Hebrews 12:12-13
Acts 20:24

Philippians 4:13
Luke 6:12
✓2 Timothy 4:7-8
Luke 13:24
✓Hebrews 10:23-24

Galatians 6:9
Mark 4:17
✓Genesis 32:26
✓Matthew 10:22
✓Acts 21:13

Questions for Discussion

1. Define what is meant by tenacity of purpose.

2. Why is fixity of purpose to be greatly valued in one's character?

3. Should one ever expect to accomplish his or her real purpose in life without being severely tested.

4. How are qualities of resolution, persistence and straight-line, deliberate action developed in one's character?

5. Is there any other joy, gladness or inward peace so wonderful as that which comes in conquering for Christ?

6. How do the spineless qualities of negligence, aimlessness, and lack of real purpose get a hold on some people?

7. Do you have goals that you will endeavor to reach with all-out, unswerving purpose?

8. Summarize the need, blessings and rewards of tenacity of purpose.

Statement: Da Vinci struggled seven long years to complete his work on "the Lord's Supper." Edison sat hour after hour, day after day, repeating "I" into a machine when sound seemed impossible to reproduce. But the will won out. Webster, with unending persistence of will, worked thirty years to finish his dictionary. Resolutions and goals mean nothing without tenacity of purpose.

Suggested Assignment

1. Memorize Philippians 4:13; 2 Timothy 2:11-13.
2. Study in depth Hebrew 12:1-13 and give a report on examples of great determination.
3. Make sentences of the following words: persistence; endurance; wavering; willpower.

Observation

Jesus said, "When it is evening, you say, 'It will be fair weather; for the sky is red.' And in the morning, 'It will be stormy today, for the sky is red and threatening.' You know how to interpret the appearance of the sky, but you cannot interpret the signs of the times" (Matthew 16:2, 3).

Observation is the act, power, or habit of seeing and noting; thorough, careful notice together with understanding.

Many times we look at something without really observing it. Observation is the ability to take account of things, and comes nearer to being a matter of habit than any of the purely mental processes. This habit can be most easily cultivated in childhood, before the mind is occupied by the problems and worries that confront the adult.

It is astonishing how much information a trained eye can grasp in a flash of time and how well it can be remembered. Regular and careful practice and an accurate checking up of the results is essential to acquiring this habit. We could make an interesting and profitable game of exercising our power of observation by looking at a picture containing a number of objects, then looking away and writing a list of as many of the objects as we can remember.

The ability to take careful notice of things is of great value to each of us, and to some it is an absolute necessity. An artist could not be an artist if he didn't possess this virtue to a fine degree. Sir Arthur Conan Doyle's famous Sherlock Holmes stories, which have entertained people for years, depend upon the great detective's ability to see things which others failed to see. The same is true of real detectives and lawyers. Scientists also rely upon this power, the

32

observation carrying with it, of course, the idea of understanding what one sees. It has been said, "The chief difference between a wise man and an ignorant one is, not that the first is acquainted with regions invisible to the second, away from common sight and interest, but that he understands the common things which the second only see."

We should begin early to train ourselves to be observant. Not only will it be useful to us in our chosen work, but it will afford us much pleasure as well.

Fill in Scriptures

1. _Matt ; 16, 3_ You know how to interpret the appearance of the sky, but you cannot interpret the signs of the times.

2. _Neh. 8 :3_ All the people were attentive to the book of the law.

3. _Acts: 17, 11_ Now these Jews were more noble than those in Thessalonica, for they received the word with eagerness, examining the scriptures daily to see if these things were so.

4. _1 Cor, 11 : 29_ For any one who eats and drinks without discerning the body eats and drinks judgment upon himself.

5. _Matt 28, 20_ Teaching them to observe all that I have commanded you; and lo, I am with you always, to the close of the age.

6. _II Cor. 13, 5_ Examine yourselves to see whether you are holding to your faith. Test yourselves.

7. _Matt: 7, 3_ Why do you see the speck that is in your brother's eye but do not notice the log that is in your own eye?

8. _II Cor 4, 4_ In their case the god of this world has blinded the minds. . . .

9. _Prov. 23, 26_ My son, give me your heart, and let your eyes observe my ways.

10. _Matt. 10, 29_ Are not two sparrows sold for a penny? And not one of them will fall to the ground without your Father's will. But even the hairs of your head are all numbered.

11. _Eph 5 :14_ Awake, O sleeper, and arise from the dead, and Christ

shall give you light. Look carefully then how you walk, not as unwise men but as wise.

12. _Acts 28:27_ For this people's heart has grown dull, and their ears are heavy of hearing, and their eyes they have closed; lest they should perceive with their eyes, and hear with their ears and understand with their heart, and turn for me to heal them.

✓ Nehemiah 8:3
✓ Matthew 10:29-30
✓ 2 Corinthians 4:4
✓ Matthew 7:3

✓ 1 Corinthians 11:29
✓ Matthew 16:3
✓ Matthew 28:20
✓ Ephesians 5:14-15

✓ Proverbs 23:26
✓ Acts 17:11
2 Corinthians 13:5
✓ Acts 28:27

Questions for Discussion

1. Define observation. _habit of seeing or notice_
2. Explain how keen observation by Paul saved a man from both physical and spiritual death (Acts 16:25-34). _The jailer_
3. Can opportunities, blessings, truth and danger sometimes stare us in the face without our being aware of them?
4. Will being observant help one to do all things well?
5. Can you name several vocations where life itself would be in great danger without keen observation?
6. How can this characteristic be a great asset to a growing church?
7. How does a person develop alertness and powers of observation?
8. Can a person become dull and boring without exercising his discerning powers?
9. Name some situations where lack of observation may seriously offend someone.
10. What is God's attitude toward the one who fails to discern the Lord's Supper?
11. What part does Satan play in distracting us and spoiling alertness, discernment and proper observation?
12. How can a person stay spiritually awake?
13. Summarize the needs, blessings, and rewards of keen observation.

Suggested Assignment

1. Memorize 1 Corinthians 11:29; Matthew 7:3
2. Take notes on the preacher's sermon.
3. Give the names of the last three persons who were baptized into Christ by your congregation.
4. How many more persons do you have at your Sunday morning services than at the evening services?

Self-Control

In teaching the Corinthian brethren to live so that they might obtain salvation, Paul said, "I buffet my body, and bring it into bondage: lest by any means, after that I have preached to others, I myself should be rejected" (1 Corinthians 9:27 ASV). Self-control is defined as control of one's own actions, impulses, desires and emotions.

Paul realized that no matter how much work he did for the Lord, if he did not have self-control he might do things which would cause him to lose the reward of salvation. If the great apostle, who suffered more and worked harder for the Lord than any other person, could realize such a need, how much more necessary it must be for us to exercise self-control.

We may be sure that this, as most other virtues, comes to us only by conscious effort, diligent practice and strong will-power. We cannot expect to acquire in a day or two the ability to remain calm and self-possessed when the storms of life beset our path, or to keep ourselves at work upon a task which may be irksome or distasteful. These traits are a part of what is meant by the term "self-control," and by constant and prayerful effort we can make self-control a part of our lives.

The ability to compel ourselves to do the right thing, when the wrong one may be more attractive and apparently offers greater rewards, is a real test of how well we are able to control our desires, acts, and emotions.

Those who have control over self will be qualified to control the endeavors and acts of others. They will be masters of the situation and pillars of strength in times when the mob is panicky and frightened. Rudyard Kipling wrote, "If you can keep your head when all about you are losing theirs and blaming it on you . . . you'll be a man, my son." We must all strive to be men in the sense of maturity in controlling self.

The person who can control himself can control any ordinary situation which may arise in life. Leonardo de Vinci said, "You can never have a greater or a less dominion than that over yourself." In developing self-control we must learn to surrender desires and wishes at the command of judgment, suppress emotions and feelings when our intelligence demands such action, submerge any rash act which may be prompted by anger, and speak kindly and lovingly when wrong is done to us. Achieving this, we will be able to say as Henley said in the poem "Invictus":

It matters not how strait the gate,
How charged with punishments the scroll,
I am the master of my fate:
I am the captain of my soul.

Man becomes a wretch without discipline. Man has the unspeakable gift of will-power by which he can do all things well in Christ. However, some persons have weak and stubborn wills that must be prodded and sometimes shocked. Man's will is his governor, his boss and king of his heart. We must surrender our will to the Divine will.

Fill in Scriptures

1. _____I pommel my body and subdue it, lest after preaching to others I myself should be disqualified.

2. _____Make every effort to supplement your . . . knowledge with self-control.

3. _____If any one thinks he is religious, and does not bridle his tongue but deceives his heart, this man's religion is vain.

4. _____Even a fool who keeps silent is considered wise; when he closes his lips, he is deemed intelligent.

5. _____Abstain from the passions of the flesh that wage war against your soul.

6. _____I say to you, Do not resist one who is evil. But if any one strike you on the right cheek, turn to him the other also.

7. _____Likewise urge the younger men to control themselves.

8._____Put a knife to your throat if you are a man given to appetite.

9._____Selfwilled, they are not afraid to speak evil of dignities.

10._____A bishop, as God's steward, must be . . . self-controlled.

11._____He was oppressed, and he was afflicted, yet he opened not his mouth; like a lamb that is led to the slaughter, and like a sheep that before its shearers is dumb, so he opened not his mouth.

12._____If your right eye causes you to sin, pluck it out and throw it away; it is better that you lose one of your members than your whole body be thrown into hell.

Matthew 5:29	Isaiah 53:7	Titus 1:7-8
2 Peter 2:10 (KJV)	Proverbs 23:2	Titus 2:6
Matthew 5:39	1 Peter 2:11	Proverbs 17:28
James 1:26	2 Peter 1:5, 6	1 Corinthians 9:27

Questions for Discussion

1. Define self-control.

2. Is this one of your strong characteristics?

3. What happens to the person who will not exercise restraint over his impulses, emotions, desires and appetites?

4. Which one of the following might be called the king or boss of your soul: the intellect, the conscience, the will or the emotions?

5. When and where is one most likely to lose self-control?

6. How important is self-control and discipline in reaching one's goals or priorities in life?

7. How does one strengthen his self-control?

8. Can you think of any worthwhile endeavor that does not require self-control?

9. How can rebuke, fear, rewards and shock sometimes help one to become a disciplined person with self-control?

10. How can the lack of discipline cause one to "sacrifice the eternal on the altar of the immediate."

11. Summarize the need, blessings, and rewards of self-control.

Suggested Assignments

1. Memorize 1 Corinthians 9:27; James 1:26.

2. Make sentences of the following words: restraint, discipline, appetites, willpower, self-control.

3. Take notes on the preacher's sermon.

4. Arise 15 minutes early each day this week to study the Scriptures.

5. Go all week without watching television or eating sweets.

6. Record the times this week that you were tempted to say something that should not have been said.

Tact

"Conduct yourselves wisely toward outsiders, making the most of the time. Let your speech always be gracious, seasoned with salt, so that you may know how you ought to answer every one" (Colossians 4:5, 6).

Tact means skill in saying and doing what is best or most suitable in given circumstances; diplomacy.

Tact depends upon the ability to understand the wishes, motives, feelings and situation of other people. It involves a desire to attain a given purpose with the least possible amount of friction or antagonism. Some people are so full of their own wishes, desires and motives that they care nothing whatever about those of other people, and are willing to over-ride them or antagonize them if necessary to secure a desired end. Tact is impossible in such a case, and only a person in a position of power can afford to be tactless. Even such a person will soon loose his friends without tact.

There are many people in this world, each with his own set of emotions, hopes, purposes, plans, etc. As we prepare to make our way through the world, and to meet and deal with others, shall we do it by forcibly pressing our will upon them and thus possibly making enemies unnecessarily? Or shall we study to ascertain their hopes and plans and then endeavor to "sell" them ours? If we choose the latter course, we must study to be tactful.

Countless thousands have failed miserably in life because they were not tactful. Important political issues have gone down in defeat because the people sponsoring them were tactless, and great causes have suffered at the hands of tactless bunglers. Wars have been lost and nations destroyed all for want of tact on the part of somebody. On the other hand, obscure people have become famous by using tact and care, with perseverance and hard work, in striving for advancement. Causes that have seemed to have little to recommend them have been advanced and given room because somebody in charge knew how to say and do the right things at the right time.

The apostle Paul was a good example of a person who had tact. To the Corinthians he wrote, "For though I am free from all men, I have made myself a slave to all, that I might win the more. To the Jews I became as a Jew, in order to win Jews; to those under the law I became as one under the law - though not being myself under the law-that I might win those under the law. To those outside the law I became as one outside the law - not being without law toward God but under the law of Christ - that I might win those outside the law. To the weak I became weak, that I might win the weak. I have become all things to all men, that I might by all means save some. I do it all for the sake of the gospel, that I may share in its blessings" (1 Corinthians 9:19-23).

The apostle was never guilty of hypocrisy, but rather showed tact in stressing that phase of his life which corresponded with those whom he would teach. Even when he had to rebuke others, which he often did because he never shirked his responsibility, he was tactful and first praised whatever good he found in their lives so they would not become too disheartened to try to do better.

It would be well for us to imitate the apostle Paul and show such tact in our dealings with others. Let us truly consider the other person, for a change, and remember that he too has feelings, hopes and plans which we might find to be even better than our own. To say the least, the better we understand the position of our associates on a matter, the more aptly and kindly we will be able to present our own will. Tact is a virtue worthy of cultivation - let us try to make it ours.

Fill in Scriptures

1. _1 Cor 14:40_ But all things should be done decently and in order.

2. _Matt 10:16_ Behold, I send you out as sheep in the midst of wolves; _1 Cor 13:4_ so be wise as serpents and innocent as doves.

3. _1 Cor_ _____ Always be prepared to make a defense to anyone who calls you to account for the hope that is in you, yet do it with gentleness and reverence.

4. _____ For we aim at what is honorable not only in the Lord's

sight but also in the sight of men.

5. _____ She is loud and wayward.

6. _____ Let your speech always be gracious, seasoned with salt, so that you may know how you ought to answer every one.

7. _____ Just as I try to please all men in everything.

8. _____ It is like sport to a fool to do wrong, but wise conduct is pleasure to a man of understanding.

9. _____ In everything a prudent man acts with knowledge, but a fool flaunts his folly.

10. _____ A fool throws off restraint and is careless.

11. _____ The King answered the people harshly, and forsaking the counsel which the old men had given him. . . .

12. _____ Love is . . . not . . . boastful . . . arrogant or rude.

13. _____ We were gentle among you, like a nurse taking care of her children.

14. _____ I preferred to do nothing without your consent in order that your goodness might not be by compulsion but of your own free will.

1 Corinthians 14:40	Proverbs 7:11	Proverbs 14:16
1 Corinthians 13:4-5	Philemon 14	Proverbs 10:23
Proverbs 13:16	Matthew 10:16	2 Corinthians 8:21
1 Corinthians 10:33	1 Peter 3:15	Colossians 4:6
1 Kings 12:13	1 Thessalonians 2:7	

Questions for Discussion

1. Define tact.

2. Do you feel this is one of your strong characteristics?

3. Would you wish to have those as your close friends who have no tact?

4. How do you feel in the presence of those who are outlandish in speech, uncouth in appearance and in every way rude?

5. Why do some snicker or whisper in the presence of the uncouth?

6. How does the lack of tact affect worship, glory of Christ and His Church?

7. How does whispering and obvious inattention in class or worship affect others?

8. Why have some developed a coarse-grained behavior?

9. Is there ever any reasonable time and place for the exercise of boisterous, rough speech and attitude?

10. How does one show or express tact by the way he dresses or by his overall appearance?

11. Does not ignorance, thoughtlessness and embarassment usually accompany one who has little tact?

12. How can we help those who are crude, unrefined and lacking in tact?

13. Since we are taught in the Scriptures to "Let all things be done in decency and in order" how can we develop better taste, and polish up abrupt manners?

14. Summarize the need, blessings and rewards of tact.

Suggested Assignments

1. Memorize 1 Corinthians 14:40; 1 Peter 3:15.

2. Make sentences of the following words: crude; tact; outlandish; uncouth; coarse-grained.

3. Observe for this week special ways that tact has been shown and make report.

Charity

"Be kind to one another, tenderhearted, forgiving one another, as God in Christ forgave you" (Ephesians 4:32).

Charity is defined as universal love and goodwill; tolerance in feeling or opinion; the disposition to think well of others; generosity to the poor; kindness; leniency.

The inward feeling of goodwill that prompts kindness in our dealings with others is called "charity." It is "love" in a broader sense of the word than love is usually supposed to include, and is developed by training and culture rather than by spontaneous attraction. Charity involves leniency in criticism, generosity of heart, and mercy which leads one to see "the other side of the question" even when it hurts one's interest to do so. A person may be charitably disposed toward those who have done him an injury, or towards classes of people whose presence and society they would be naturally inclined to shun.

No man is truly educated, no matter how much he knows, until he is charitable, in his thoughts and sentiments. Charity helps us to realize that others have worthwhile qualities and to feel with them in their troubles. It is this virtue which helps erase the boundaries of class, nation and race, and leads to a sense of the brotherhood of all men. Charity does away with snobbishness and bigotry. It has been said, "The only hope of preserving what is best lies in the practice of an immense charity, a wide tolerance, a sincere respect for opinions that are not ours."

Charity is closely akin to mercy; indeed, mercy is one phase or branch of charity, being that part which shows leniency. We might show leniency of opinion regarding some wrong done us, and kindness to the offender such as kindness toward animals or those weaker than ourselves. Queen Victoria said, "No civilization is complete which does not include the dumb and defenseless of God's creatures within the sphere of charity and mercy."

We must keep ourselves from slighting remarks, gossip, open criticism of others, and all such things which show a lack of charity. Whenever possible we can express, either by word or act, sentiments that are loving and charitable. If we knew each other better perhaps there would be more understanding and charity and less criticism.

Each of us can make this troubled world a better place by developing and practicing charity in our own lives.

Fill in Scriptures

1. _____In all things I have shown you that by so toiling one must help the weak, remembering the words of the Lord Jesus, how he said, "It is more blessed to give than to receive."

2. _____But I say to you, Love your enemies and pray for those who persecute you, so that you may be sons of your Father who is in heaven; for he makes his sun rise on the evil and on the good.

3. _____But if any one has the world's goods and sees his brother in need, yet closes his heart against him, how does God's love abide in him?

4. _____If I speak in the tongues of men and of angels, but have not love, I am a noisy gong or a clanging cymbal.

5. _____For I could wish that I myself were accursed and cut off from Christ for the sake of my brethren.

6. _____We who are strong ought to bear with the failings of the weak, and not to please ourselves; let each of us please his neighbor. . . .

7. _____For if you forgive men their trespasses, your heavenly Father also will forgive you.

8. _____Better is a dinner of herbs where love is than a fatted ox and hatred with it.

9. _____But God shows his love for us in that while we were yet sinners Christ died for us.

10. _____Honor all men.

11. _____He brought me to the banqueting house, and his banner

over me was love.

12._____Associate with the lowly; never be conceited. Repay no
one evil for evil, but take thought for what is noble in
the sight of all. If possible, so far as it depends upon you,
live peaceably with all.

Matthew 6:14	Romans 15:1-2	Romans 9:3
1 Corinthians 13:1	1 John 3:17	Romans 12:16-18
Song of Solomon 2:4	1 Peter 2:17	Romans 5:8
Matthew 5:44-45	Proverbs 15:17	Acts 20:35

Questions for Discussion

1. Define charity.

2. Does the church where you attend have a spirit of benevolence and goodwill toward all humanity?

3. What are your benevolent programs?

4. Do you manifest a strong affection to your parents, brothers and sisters with an active interest in all they do or say?

5. Do you show lenient judgment toward the offenses and faults of others?

6. Do you hold a grudge?

7. Do you try to push your responsiblities on to others?

8. Are you envious of other people's abilities and blessings?

9. Do you commit murder by hating someone?

10. Do you hold resentment?

11. Do you make excuses for missing worship services?

12. Are you enslaved to a bad habit that wrecks your mind, body and soul, one that spoils your influence as a Christian?

13. Have you placed other interests before God?

14. Have you blamed others for your own failures?

15. Have you used your time in the right way?

16. Are you fault-finding of others?

17. Are you willing to follow?

18. Have you cheated someone?

19. Are you really interested in making a happy home?

20. Have you spoken unkindly to someone?

Suggested Assignments

1. Memorize Acts 20:35; Matthew 5:44, 45.

2. Make sentences of the following words: benevolence; helfulness; liberality; charity.

3. Send a card of sympathy to a family of a deceased one. If necessary, use the obituary column of the newspaper.

Thoroughness

The apostle Paul warned the Corinthians, "Do you not know that in a race all the runners compete, but only one receives the prize? So run that you may obtain it" (1 Corinthians 9:24).

Thoroughness is defined as the quality of going on to the end; completing that which is begun; finishing; not being superficial.

This is a quality lacking in many people, but you may be sure that the successful individuals of this world do possess it. It is a virtue which can hardly be overemphasized as a characteristic desirable in both children and adults. Much of the loss and destruction so often seen is due to the fact that somebody has not been thorough in his work. We see examples of this in the collapse of large structures such as buildings, bridges and the like. Erosion, floods and forest fires are usually due to a lack of thoroughness; someone did their work carelessly and without finishing that which was necessary to prevent such catastrophes. Too often a person's failure in life is due to the fact that he was not thorough in his preparation for it. We must never be content with substitutes in place of genuine moral or mental material for our life-structure. To be content with results that are merely "good enough" rather than to do our "level best" and make it our standard of life, is to take the road to failure, if not complete disaster.

The Bible exhorts Christians to thoroughness so that their work may be acceptable in the sight of God. The apostle Paul wrote to the Philippians, "I am sure that he who began a good work in you will bring it to completion at the day of Jesus Christ" (Philippians 1:6). And to the Corinthians, "In this matter, I give my advice: it is best for you now to complete what a year ago you began not only to do but to desire, so that your readiness in desiring it may be matched by your completing it out of what you have" (2 Corinthians 8:10,11). Again we read, "Awake, and strengthen what remains and is on the point of death, for I have not found your works perfect in the sight of my God" (Revelation 3:2).

Seeing how much this quality of being thorough means to us, whether it be in the preparing for or the doing of our work, and above all, how much it means to us in our preparation for life eternal, let us practice it in each thing that we do. Daily practice of this virtue will make it a habit, and a part of our character which we will find most profitable.

Fill in Scriptures

1. _____And every work that he undertook in the service of the house of God and in accordance with the law and the commandments, seeking his God, he did with all his heart, and prospered.

2. _____You wicked and slothful servant! You knew that I reaped where I have not sowed, and gather where I have not winnowed? Then you ought to have invested my money with the bankers, and at my coming I should have received what was my own with interest.

3. _____For which of you, desiring to build a tower, does not first sit down and count the cost, whether he has enough to complete it? Otherwise, when he has laid the foundation, and is not able to finish, all who see it began to mock him.

4. _____I have fought the good fight, I have finished the race, I have kept the faith. Henceforth there is laid up for me a crown of righteousness.

5. _____I did not shrink from declaring to you anything that was profitable, and teaching you in public and from house to house.

6. _____Awake, and strengthen what remains and is on the point of death, for I have not found your works perfect in the sight of my God.

7. _____Ephraim mixes himself with the peoples; Ephraim is a cake not turned.

8. _____Go therefore and make disciples . . . teaching them to observe all that I have commanded you.

9. _____For truly, I say to you, till heaven and earth pass away, not an iota, not a dot, will pass from the law until all is accomplished.

10. _____But even the hairs of your head are all numbered.

11. _____All the people answered with one voice. . . "All the words which the Lord has spoken we will do."

12. _____I know your works, your love and faith and service and patient endurance, and that your latter works exceed the first.

Matthew 25:26-27	Revelation 3:2	Hosea 7:8
Exodus 24:3	Revelation 2:19	2 Chronicles 31:21
Luke 14:28-29	2 Timothy 4:7-8	Acts 20:20
Matthew 28:19-20	Matthew 10:30	Matthew 5:18

Questions For Discussion

1. Define thoroughness.

2. How important is it that we commend those who have done well?

3. Can the attitude that any performance is good enough stir the wrath of God?

4. How can slothfulness and carelessness to details spoil programs of the church?

5. Is thoroughness mostly a natural quality or one that is developed?

6. Why, as a rule, will only a few volunteer for activities that require painstaking effort?

7. Have you observed any programs or activities that have not been carried through to completion?

8. Is one to be pitied, rebuked or encouraged that has failed to complete an assignment?

9. What feeling does one experience who has properly and thoroughly completed a worthy project?

10. Name some programs or projects that require cooperation and team effort before they can be completed with success.

11. Summarize the need, blessings and rewards of thoroughness.

Suggested Assignments

1. Memorize Ecclesiastes 9:10.
2. Take time to go out of your way to commend someone who is doing an excellent work for the Lord.
3. Make a list of good works that you have finished and have done well for the Lord.
4. Suggest a project that you wish to see begun and completed.

Carefulness

The apostle Paul wrote to Titus, "I desire you to insist on these things, so that those who have believed in God may be **careful** to apply themselves to good deeds; these are excellent and profitable to men" (Titus 3:8).

Carefulness means to give thoughtful attention to details; to exercise forethought, prudence, watchfulness and discretion.

Carefulness, like thinking, is difficult to practice unless we make it a habit, and not everyone possesses this very important characteristic. To acquire this habit we must center our mind on what is being done, use caution as to how it is done, have concern as to the result, and be watchful and careful throughout the process.

Many people are satisfied if the work they do is just "good enough," but to merely do "good enough" work, means that the person will never try to do his best. That person will never become trained in those little habits of carefulness that make up real ability. To do any work well, it is necessary to give thoughtful attention to the small details; this done, the work as a whole will be done to the best of that person's ability.

We can train ourselves in carefulness by giving thought for the many little things we do daily. Do we allow doors to slam, instead of closing them quietly? When we are eating do we chew with our mouth closed? Are we considerate to pass food to others at the table? When we are walking on the sidewalk, do we allow room for other people to pass us without their being crowded off the walk? Do we allow others to finish what they are saying before we start to speak, or do we interrupt their conversation?

It might be of real value for us to make a list of our good and bad habits, in order to correct the bad ones and thus begin cultivating the habit of carefulness.

Fill in Scriptures

1. _____ Observe carefully what is before you.

2. _____ "And if you obey the voice of the Lord your God, being careful to do all his commandments which I command you this day, the Lord your God will set you high above all the nations of the earth. And all these blessings shall come upon you. . . .

3. _____ Look carefully then how you walk, not as unwise men but as wise, making the most of the time, because the days are evil.

4. _____ Therefore let anyone who thinks that he stands take heed lest he fall.

5. _____ Be sober, be watchful. Your adversary the devil prowls around like a roaring lion, seeking some one to devour.

6. _____ But we were gentle among you, like a nurse taking care of her children.

7. _____ The saying is sure. I desire you to insist on these things, so that those who have believed in God may be careful to apply themselves to good deeds.

8. _____ See to it that no one makes a prey of you by philosophy and empty deceit, according to human tradition. . . .

9. _____ Be not like a horse or a mule, without understanding, which must be curbed with bit and bridle, else it will not keep with you.

10. _____ Only be strong and very courageous, being careful to do according to all the law which Moses my servant commanded you; turn not from it to the right hand or to the left, that you may have good success wherever you go.

11. _____ Moses was about to erect the tent, he was instructed by God, saying, "See that you make everything according to the pattern which was shown you on the mountain.

12. _____ How shall we escape if we neglect such a great salvation?

Hebrews 8:5	Joshua 1:7	Psalms 32:9
Colossians 2:8	Titus 3:8	1 Thessalonians 2:7
1 Peter 5:8	1 Corinthians 10:12	Hebrews 2:3
Ephesians 5:15-16	Deuteronomy 28:1-2	Proverbs 23:1

Questions for Discussion

1. Define carefulness.
2. What does carefulness reveal about one's attitude?
3. How does attentive concern in Bible class effect teacher and student?
4. What is God's attitude toward careless men?
5. Is there any endeavor really worthwhile that does not require carefulness?
6. How does carelessness adversely affect friendship, the home, the church, driving a car, or one's vocation?
7. Does God require anything less than careful painstaking effort on the part of a Christian?
8. Tell of some tragedy that happened because caution was thrown to the wind.
9. How do the sloven attitudes of indifferent Christians effect the church?
10. How costly is it to be careless in discerning the Lord's supper? (1 Corinthians 11:29, 30).
11. Summarize the need, blessings and rewards of carefulness.

Suggested Assignments

1. Memorize Ephesians 5:15, 16; Titus 3:8.
2. Make sentences of the following words: carefulness, caution, sloven, heedless, attentive, negligence.
3. Clip from the newspaper an article that gives a report on some act of carelessness that caused a needless accident.

Self-Judgment

The Apostle Paul wrote to the Roman brethren, "I bid every one among you not to think of himself more highly than he ought to think, but to think with sober judgment. . . ." (Romans 12:3).

Self-judgment is a careful inspection of, or scrutiny into, one's own conduct, thoughts, beliefs, motives, etc., with a view to regulating them.

It is important that we be well-acquainted with self and that we understand our strong qualities so that we may use them effectively. Self-judgment is not only our ability to understand our own thoughts, words and actions, but it is also the ability to decide rightly what we should do, what we should say, and what we should be, during life.

To the Corinthians Paul wrote, "Examine yourselves, to see whether you are holding to your faith. Test yourselves" (2 Corinthians 13:5). It is well for each of us to examine ourselves frequently and to judge whether we are holding to the course we have set. It is much easier to see the other person's faults than to see our own, because we are often lacking in self-judgment. In Galatians 6:1 we read, "Brethren, if a man is overtaken in any trespass, you who are spiritual should restore him in a spirit of gentleness. Look to yourself, lest you too be tempted."

If we will examine ourselves and judge our condition to the best of our ability, it will seldom be necessary for others to condemn us in the things we do or say. Self-judgment, properly and frequently applied, can earn for each of us the respect of those about us.

The Lord has set aside a special time each week for each Christian to examine himself. "Let a man examine himself and so eat of the bread and drink of the cup'' (1 Corinthians 11:28). This, of course, is to be done while taking of the Lord's Supper. There are other important aspects of this feast. However, examining oneself is vital if one expects to please the Lord while in worship. Even though we may examine ourselves many times through the week, there is a special weekly examination to be made on each first day of the week as we assemble together. This suggests to us the Lord's estimate of self-examination or self-judgment!

This tends to humble us when we compare ourselves with Christ. And "if we judged ourselves truly, we should not be judged" (1 Corinthians 11:31 RSV).

Also the scriptures stress that we must use the right standard in self-judgment. "Not that we venture to class or compare ourselves with some of those who commend themselves. But when they measure themselves by one another, and compare themselves with one another, they are without understanding" (2 Corinthians 10:12).

Fill in Scriptures

1. _____The Pharisee stood and prayed thus with himself, "God, I thank thee that I am not like other men."

2. _____I bid every one among you not to think of himself more highly than he ought to think.

3. _____Let a man examine himself.

4. _____The way of a fool is right in his own eyes.

5. _____Count others better than yourselves.

6. _____Lord, I am not worthy to have you come under my roof.

7. _____I am the foremost of sinners.

8. _____"He must increase, but I must decrease."

9. _____Search me, O God, and know my heart! Try me and know my thoughts! And see if there be any wicked way in me.

10. _____Not that we are sufficient of ourselves to claim anything as coming from us; our sufficiency is from God.

11. _____Be not wise in your own eyes.

12. _____Therefore let any one who thinks he stands take heed lest he fall.

Romans 12:3	Philippians 2:3	Proverbs 3:7
Matthew 8:8	1 Timothy 1:15	1 Corinthians 10:12
2 Corinthians 3:5	Luke 18:11	1 Corinthians 11:28
Proverbs 12:15	John 3:30	Psalms 139:23, 24

Questions for Discussion

1. Define self-judgment.
2. Do you feel this is one of your strong characteristics?
3. What is the purpose of self-judgment?
4. "What kind of a church would this church be if every member were just like me?"
5. Why is it easier to see the weaknesses and faults of others more readily than in our selves?
6. Some think too highly of themselves and become inflated and proud, while others think too little of themselves and wither away to become a "nobody." In your opinion which of the two weaknesses is the most disasterous?
7. We are taught in the Scriptures to examine ourselves. What are we to really search for?
8. How would others feel toward us if they really knew us as well as we know ourselves?
9. In Philippians 2:3 we are taught to count others better than ourselves. Should this be difficult?
10. Does it bother you deeply to have others criticize you?
11. What are the needs, blessings and rewards of self-judgment?

Suggested Assignments

1. Memorize Romans 12:3; Proverbs 12:15.
2. Make sentences of the following words: self-judgment; examination; soul-searching; self-righteous.
3. List improvements you wish to make in your life.
4. Try to list for today all your thoughts, words and deeds that you are ashamed of.
5. Give written or oral report on the two men that went up to the temple to pray.

Hospitality

"Let brotherly love continue. Do not neglect to show hospitality to strangers, for thereby some have entertained angels unawares" (Hebrews 13:1, 2).

Hospitality is the practice of entertaining friends or strangers with kindness and liberality.

Much is said in God's Word regarding hospitality, both in the Old and in the New Testaments. From the beginning it has been God's will that man practice hospitality toward his fellowman. The many examples shown, and the exhortations to practice it, can leave no doubt in our mind that this is a virtue we would do well to weave into the cloth of our life.

The opening verse refers to a time when Abraham unknowingly entertained angels by practicing hospitality to strangers. The Shunammite woman, who, with her husband, prepared a room for Elisha to lodge in whenever he came their way, was another notable example of hospitality. Matthew, the publican, made a great feast for Jesus; and Lydia, the seller of purple in the city of Thyatira, lodged Paul and his fellow workers in her house while they were in the city where she lived. Paul, and the others shipwrecked with him on the Island of Melita, were treated hospitably by the people who lived there. These are only a few of the examples of hospitality recorded in the Bible. Each is a testimonial of man's kindness to man. How different it is from the war, hate and greed that fills so much of the world.

The apostle Peter admonished Christians to "Above all hold unfailing your love for one another, since love covers a multitude of sins. Practice hospitality ungrudgingly to one another. As each has

60

received a gift, employ it for one another" (1 Peter 4:8-10). The apostle Paul told the Romans to "Contribute to the needs of the saints, practice hospitality" (Romans 12:13).

Each of us would do well to practice hospitality whenever the opportunity presents itself, as this is truly one of the great fruits of the spirit.

Fill in Sentences

1. _____And the natives showed us unusual kindness, for they kindled a fire and welcomed us all, because it had begun to rain and was cold.

2. _____The stranger who sojourns with you shall be to you as the native among you, and you shall love him as yourself.

3. _____Contribute to the needs of the saints, practice hospitality.

4. _____Do not neglect to show hospitality to strangers, for thereby some have entertained angels unaware.

5. _____Two angels came to Sodom . . . and Lot was sitting in the gate of Sodom. When Lot saw them, he rose to meet them, and bowed himself with his face to the earth, and said, "My lords, turn aside, I pray you, to your servants house and spend the night, and wash your feet; then you may rise up early and go on your way."

6. _____He (Reuel) said to his daughters, "And where is he? Why have you left the man? Call him, that he may eat bread."

7. _____Practice hospitality ungrudgingly to one another.

8. _____Now a bishop must be . . . hospitable.

9. _____Religion that is pure and undefiled . . . is this: to visit orphans and widows in their affliction, and to keep oneself unstained in the world.

10. _____He (Laban) said, "Come in . . . why do you stand outside? For I have prepared the house. . ." Then food was set before him to eat.

11. _____Let us make a small roof chamber with walls, and put there for him a bed, a table, a chair, and a lamp, so that whenever he comes to us, he can go in there.

Romans 12:13   Hebrews 13:2   1 Timothy 3:2
2 Kings 4:10   Leviticus 19:34   Exodus 2:20
James 1:27   Genesis 24:31-33   Acts 28:2
Genesis 19:1-2   1 Peter 4:9

Questions for Discussion

1. Define hospitality.
2. Do you feel that it is one of your strong characteristics?
3. Would you wish to be associated with, married to, in business with, or active in any other endeavor with those who disregard hospitality?
4. Who is most responsible in fulfilling God's Word in making this world a warm and friendly place to live?
5. Is the church where you attend known for its fine hospitality to strangers?
6. Who needs the healing touch of attention the most?
7. When did you last go out of your way to be friendly and hospitable to a stranger?
8. What do a stewardess, a waitress, and a receptionist have in common?
9. Are smiles, facial expressions and handshakes a universal language?
10. Name some very effective ways to show hospitality on the street where you live; at worship services; at school or college.
11. Why do people like to be shown hospitality?
12. Why are some people cold, snobbish, or unhospitable?
13. Are all people at times lonely?
14. Since the literal meaning of hospitality is to "love strangers" summarize the need, blessings, and rewards of hospitality. Suggest special ways that it must be done.

Suggested Assignments

1. Memorize Romans 12:13; 1 Peter 4:9; James 1:27.
2. Invite someone into your home, preferably one whom you don't know very well.

3. Go out of your way to show friendship to some visitor at church.

4. Make sentences with the following words: snobbish; hospitality; self-centered; unfriendly.

5. Give a full report on Genesis 18:1-8.

Gratitude

We read in Ephesians 5:20, "Always and for everything giving thanks in the name of our Lord Jesus Christ to God the Father."

Gratitude is the state of being thankful; appreciation of favors received; response to kindness.

One of the most admirable traits a person can have is that of a well-developed sense of gratitude. It has been said, "No man is in true health who can not stand in the free air of heaven, with his feet on God's free turf, and thank his Creator for the simple luxury of physical existence."

Thoughtfulness is one of the primary factors in developing a sense of gratitude. We must first take note of the fact that someone has done us a favor or kindness. Then, having done that, we must recognize the spirit of consideration which prompted the act. When the full significance of the situation is impressed upon our mind we can hardly fail to feel appreciation for the kindness and gratitude to the one by whom it was given.

Paul told the Thessalonians to: "Rejoice always, pray constantly, give thanks in all circumstances; for this is the will of God in Christ Jesus for you" (1 Thessalonians 5:16-18). Christians should be the most thankful people on earth, realizing with gratitude that God, our Creator, has given us everything we need for a good life here, and the promise of life eternal through his Son, if we will but obey him. Every command of his has been for our own good, both here and in the hereafter, and yet we so often fail to appreciate God's blessings.

Each of us has been aware of the feeling of disgust when seeing someone accept a kindness with no apparent sense of gratitude.

Let us carefully consider our lives and its many blessings and not be guilty of taking them for granted. Remember how many times others do things to make our lives more comfortable and pleasant. Our parents, our family, friends and associates all do many little acts of service to help us through each day. Let us ask ourselves, are we really grateful? Most of all, are we grateful to our Heavenly Father for the blessings he has given us? We could hardly help having a feeling of gratitude in our hearts if we would really take the time and think on these expressions of love extended to us by others.

Fill in Scriptures

1. _____If you will not listen, if you will not lay it to heart to give glory to my name, says the Lord of hosts, then I will send the curse upon you and I will curse your blessings.

2. _____For everything created by God is good, and nothing is to be rejected if it is received with thanksgiving.

3. _____Because you did not serve the Lord your God with joyfulness and gladness of heart, by reason of the abundance of all things, therefore you shall serve your enemies whom the Lord will send against you.

4. _____For although they knew God they did not honor him as God or give thanks to him, but they became futile in their thinking and their senseless minds were darkened.

5. _____Through him then let us continually offer up a sacrifice of praise to God, that is, the fruit of lips that acknowledge his name.

6. _____Enter his gates with thanksgiving, and his courts with praise! Give thanks to him, bless his name!

7. _____Always and for everything giving thanks in the name of our Lord.

8. _____And they shall stand every morning, thanking and praising the Lord, and likewise at evening.

9. _____Jesus said, "Was no one found to return and give praise to God except this foreigner?"

10. _____Let everything that breathes praise the Lord.

11._____At midnight I rise to praise thee, because of thy righteous ordinances.

12._____Then we thy people, the flock of thy pasture, will give thanks to thee forever.

1 Timothy 4:4	Hebrews 13:15	Ephesians 5:20
Psalms 79:13	Luke 17:18	Malachi 2:2
Romans 1:21	Psalms 100:4	1 Chronicles 23:30
Deuteronomy 28:47-48	Psalms 150:6	Psalms 119:62

Questions for Discussion

1. Define gratitude.
2. Do you feel that a spirit of gratitude is one of your strong characteristics?
3. Would you wish to be married to a person, or associated with any group that lacks deep gratitude?
4. Make a list of the 10 greatest blessings you have received.
5. Do you believe that you continually and adequately express gratitude for your blessings?
6. What book of the Bible expresses thanksgiving more than any other?
7. Why are men prone to vaguely feel or appreciate divine grace?
8. What are some of the penalties for being an ingrate?
9. What did the apostle Paul mean when he said, "What have you that you did not receive?" (1 Corinthians 4:7).
10. Do you feel that our worship in songs, prayers and sermons have been adequate to express due gratitude to God?
11. Why didn't the nine lepers return to give glory to God?
12. Which do you feel is man's greater weakness—to properly receive blessings or give blessings?
13. Is it possible for one to be happy or wise without expressing gratitude?
14. Is it more joyous to receive or give blessings and gifts?
15. Summarize the need, blessings and rewards of gratitude.

Suggested Assignments

1. Memorize Philippians 4:4; 1 Timothy 4:4.

2. Make sentences using the following words: ingrate; thanksgiving; blessings; praise; joy.

3. Express gratitude to parents, friends, elders, or preacher for blessings received.

Honesty

"Whatever is true, whatever is honorable, whatever is just, whatever is pure, whatever is lovely, whatever is gracious, if there is any excellence, if there is anything worthy of praise, think about these things" (Philippians 4:8).

Honesty is defined as the quality of being free from deceit. It is straightforwardness, fairness, sincerity, and truth. Honesty is that quality of man that shows him fair and truthful in speech, above cheating, stealing, misrepresentation, or any other fraudulent action.

Honesty means being fair with our fellow man and with ourselves. It means paying our obligations promptly, whether the debt is one of money, service, opinion, friendly advice, living up to the rules of the game we play, or writing an examination fairly. If we are honest in all matters, we will build into our characters one of life's greatest attributes, and establish a good reputation. We have all heard the proverb, "Honesty is the best policy" and we know that it means we will profit most by being honest.

We should be honest in our every thought, word, and act, then we will have the confidence, respect, and admiration of others. Without honesty we could not have their respect and confidence, and there would be little opportunity for us to achieve true success.

Paul wrote to the Corinthians, that in taking the money for the relief of the poor Christians in Jerusalem, he was aiming "at what is honorable not only in the Lord's sight but also in the sight of men" (2 Corinthians 8:21).

We should do as Paul did, and remember that we must also be honest in all things, both in the sight of the Lord and of men. Through daily practice we can acquire this wonderful characteristic.

68

Fill in Scriptures

1. _____A false witness will not go unpunished, and he who utters lies will perish.

2. _____Do not add to his words, lest he rebuke you, and you be found a liar.

3. _____As for you, you whitewash with lies.

4. _____Because you have said, "We have made a covenant with death . . . we have made lies our refuge, and in falsehood we have taken shelter;"

5. _____You are of your father the devil . . . there is no truth in him. When he lies, he speaks according to his own nature, for he is a liar and the father of lies.

6. _____No man who practices deceit shall dwell in my house; no man who utters lies shall continue in my presence.

7. _____"Why has Satan filled your heart to lie. . . You have not lied to men but to God." When Ananias heard these words, he fell down and died.

8. _____But as for the cowardly, . . . and all liars, their lot shall be in the lake that burns with fire.

9. _____The Spirit expressly says that in later times some will depart from the faith by giving heed to deceitful spirits and doctrines of demons, through the pretensions of liars whose consciences are seared.

10. _____We have renounced disgraceful, underhanded ways; we refuse to practice cunning or to tamper with God's word, but by the open statement of the truth we would commend ourselves to every man's conscience in the sight of God.

11. _____Thy words were found, and I ate them.

12. _____There are six things which the Lord hates . . . haughty eyes, a lying tongue, and hands that shed innocent blood, a heart that devises wicked plans, feet that make haste to run to evil, a false witness who breathes out lies.

Proverbs 30:6   Job 13:4   John 8:44
Revelations 21:8   Proverbs 19:9   Isaiah 28:15
Psalms 101:7   Acts 5:3-5   1 Timothy 4:1-2
2 Corinthians 4:2 Jeremiah 15:16   Proverbs 6:16-19

Questions for Discussion

1. Define honesty.

2. When is one most likely to be tempted to be deceitful?

3. Why are we attracted to persons who are straightforward, frank, sincere and completely honest?

4. How does dishonesty affect our conscience, our friends, our God and our future?

5. What should our attitude be toward one who lacks integrity?

6. What is a half-truth, and how can it be more dangerous than an outright black lie?

7. Where is innocence, respectability and credability most disregarded?

8. Can exaggeration, flattery, and overstatements ever be justified?

9. Is it ever easy to gain trust in one who has deceived you?

10. When can neutrality and silence become hypocritical and dishonest?

11. How do some temporarily avoid suffering and embarrassment by cheating and lying?

12. Summarize the need, blessings and rewards of honesty.

Suggested Assignments

1. Memorize Proverbs 6:16-19; Proverbs 19:9.

2. Make sentences of the following words: honesty; deceit; exaggeration; truth; lie; integrity.

3. Study 1 Kings 13 and report how a young man lost his life for believing a lie.

Helpfulness

"Bear one another's burdens, and so fulfill the law of Christ" (Galatians 6:2).

Helpfulness is the quality of being useful or of service; giving aid or assistance. This is the spirit of kindness and loving co-operation, of being of service and helping our friends and associates to enjoy life in some way to a greater degree than would otherwise be possible. We can be helpful to others through kind words or loving deeds, or by doing our own work efficiently and well. Perhaps a friendly suggestion or relating some facts pertinent to the situation would be of service to another. It would be impossible to name the hundreds of opportunities we will have during life to be useful to others, but it is important that we help at every opportunity.

Jesus told his disciples when they disputed among themselves as to who should be the greatest, "If any man desire to be first, the same shall be last of all, and servant of all" (Mark 9:35). And the apostle Paul wrote, "We who are strong ought to bear with the failings of the weak, and not to please ourselves; let each of us please his neighbor for his good, to edify him" (Romans 15:1, 2). It is a great and valuable truth that a person's success in life is in proportion to his helpfulness and service to others.

We cannot begin too early in life to cultivate a spirit of helpfulness. Too often we are content to let someone else wait upon us, and we fail to accept our responsibilities. The first step toward helping others is, then, to learn to help one's self; to do the work for which we are responsible both promptly and to be best of our ability.

There is a very real joy in doing something for somebody else, and if we can train ourselves to think of the things to be done ourselves, rather than having to wait to be told what to do and how to do it, our pleasure will be increased. Helpfulness is one of the marks of a true Christian, and will do much bring happiness to both ourselves and those about us; but, more than that, it pleases God that we be helpful to others.

Fill in Scriptures

1. _____Bear one another's burdens, and so fulfil the law of Christ.

2. _____Every one helps his neighbor, and says to his brother, "Take courage!"

3. _____A Samaritan. . .came. . .and bound up his wounds, pouring on oil and wine; then he set him on his own beast and brought him to an inn, and took care of him.

4. _____Through love be servants of one another.

5. _____You also must help us by prayer, so that many will give thanks on our behalf for the blessing granted us in answer to many prayers.

6. _____If your enemy is hungry, feed him; if he is thirsty, give him a drink.

7. _____Let us consider how to stir up one another to love and good works. . .encouraging one another.

8. _____I do not mean that others should be eased and you burdened, but that as a matter of equality your abundance at the present time should supply their want, so that their abundance may supply your want, that there may be equality.

9. _____You yourselves know that these hands ministered to my necessities, and to those who were with me. In all things I have shown you that by so toiling one must help the weak, remembering the words of the Lord Jesus, how he said, "It is more blessed to give than receive."

10._____I commend to you our sister Phoebe, a deaconess of the church at Cenchreae, that you may receive her in the Lord as befits the saints, and help her in whatever she may require from you, for she has been a helper of many and of myself as well.

11. _____I have no one like him, who will be genuinely anxious for your welfare. They all look after their own interests ... .But Timothy's worth you know, how as a son with a father he has served with me in the gospel.

Galatians 5:13   2 Corinthians 1:11   Isaiah 41:6
Hebrews 10:24-25   Philippians 2:20-22   Galatians 6:2
Luke 10:33-34   Romans 12:20   2 Corinthians 8:13-14
Acts 20:34-35   Romans 16:1-2

Questions for Discussion

1. Define helpfulness.
2. Tell of an experience you had in helping someone with an overload?
3. Do you share in everday chores about the house?
4. Have you ever volunteered assistance to a worthy church program?
5. How do you feel toward those who purposely avoid or shirk responsibility?
6. Have you ever tried to prevent a good program from failing?
7. Do you make it a habit to compliment those who are being helpful to others?
8. Are you happier when serving others or being served?
9. On what programs of the church are you sharing your time and energy?
10. Do you try to be alert to and observant of the needs of others?
11. Do others feel that they can call on you in their time of need?
12. Do you resent or try to avoid responsibility?
13. Do you feel that others look upon you as one who is positive, having an optimistic attitude, or one who is negative?
14. Are you willing to stick your neck out for the Lord?
15. Summarize the need, blessings, and rewards of helpfulness.

Suggested Assignments

1. Memorize Isaiah 41:6; Hebrews 10:24, 25.
2. Make sentences of the following words: share; helpful; assist; support.

3. Ask your leaders, teachers, elders or parents how you can become more involved in active service.

4. Ask some widow or aged person if they need help with some chore about their home or residence and volunteer your services.

Proper Thinking

"Whatever is true, whatever is honorable, whatever is just, whatever is pure, whatever is lovely, whatever is gracious, if there is any excellence, if there is anything worthy of praise, think about these things" (Philippians 4:8).

Thought is defined as the act or process of mental activity; meditation reflection; that which the mind conceives, considers, or imagines; an idea or intention.

Although they may never assume physical or material being, thoughts are things and are the basis of all human achievement. The ability to think carefully upon the problems of life helps our judgment in selecting the proper course to pursue.

In developing this quality, it is important that we give consideration to the information obtained upon each subject before us. Thought calls forth our ability to arrange facts and duly weigh them in order that we may choose the good and eliminate the evil.

King Solomon said, "As a man thinketh in his heart, so is he" (Proverbs 23:7 KJV). How careful we should be of our thoughts to keep them pure, honorable and lovely as the apostle Paul admonished the Philippians.

Thomas Carlyle, the Scottish writer, said, "The thought is parent of the deed, nay, is living soul of it." If we allow our thoughts to dwell on evil it will show in the things we do and say. We are the only ones who can control our thoughts, although others may help us by contributing facts for our consideration. We must always carefully weigh these facts in the light of God's Word, using his principles regarding good and evil to help us think out our course of action.

You are what you think. Thoughts are the blueprints for action, and the "parents of the deed." By a process of thought-control man becomes what he choses to be. Thoughts can be living and active—more powerful than dynamite and even more destructive. Thoughts can lift a man to the extreme height of joy and goodness. In the final analysis each man is responsible for his thoughts. He is just as strong or as weak or as good as his thoughts. If we radically change our thinking, we radically change the circumstances of our life. We are to think God's thoughts as revealed in the scriptures. This will bring a joyful, useful life now and in the hereafter. "Be transformed by the renewal of your mind" (Romans 12:1). Destructive habit patterns in thinking must be put down and replaced by that which is pure, constructive and positive. We must strive for the most noble thoughts possible to be happy and successful.

Fill in Scriptures

1. _____As he thinketh in his heart, so is he.

2. _____Be transformed by the renewal of your mind.

3. _____Brethren, do not be children in your thinking; be babes in evil, but in thinking be mature.

4. _____My thoughts are not your thoughts, neither are your ways my ways.

5. _____The Lord knows the thoughts of man, that they are but a breath.

6. _____Take heed lest there be a base thought in your heart.

7. _____But his delight is in the law of the Lord, and on his law he meditates day and night. He is like a tree planted by streams of water, that yields its fruit in its season. . . In all that he does, he prospers.

8. _____The Lord saw that the wickedness of man was great in the earth, and that every imagination of the thoughts of his heart was only evil continually. And the Lord was sorry that he had made man on earth, and it grieved him to his heart.

9. _____Finally, brethren, whatever is true, whatever is honorable, whatever is just, whatever is pure, whatever is lovely, whatever is gracious, if there is any excellence, if there

is anything worthy of praise, think about these things.
. . . And the God of peace will be with you.

10._____We . . . take every thought captive to obey Christ.

11._____Search me, O God, and know my heart! Try me and
know my thoughts! And see if there be any wicked way
in me.

12._____When I was a child, I spoke like a child, I thought like
a child, I reasoned like a child; when I became a man,
I gave up childish ways.

Proverbs 23:7 (KJV)	Philippians 4:8-9	Psalms 139:23-24
Isaiah 55:8	1 Corinthians 14:20	Psalms 94:11
1 Corinthians 13:11	Deuteronomy 15:9	Genesis 6:5-6
Romans 12:2	Psalms 1:2-3	2 Corinthians 10:5

Questions for Discussion

1. Define proper thinking.
2. How can thinking affect our emotions and even our bodies?
3. What happens to the person who habitually dwells on negative thoughts?
4. How does one develop thought control?
5. Does the mind grow on what it feeds?
6. Can the outward conditions and circumstances of one's life reflect one's process of thinking, and if so, how?
7. How many thoughts is it possible for one to think at a time?
8. How do positive, hopeful thoughts affect one's personality?
9. What part does willpower play upon one's thinking?
10. When a person radically changes his thinking what happens to his or her life?
11. Is it right to say a person is just as strong or weak or good as his thoughts?
12. How does Satan attempt to short-circuit our brain as to block out a pure, clean, smooth flow of intellectual powers?
13. Will acute drainage of brain power exist when the will becomes weak or fails to discipline the intellect?

14. The Creator of the heart designed the mind to think God's thoughts after him; how is this to be done?

15. Name some of the endless list of things that seek to bombard the mind like an onrushing flood such as television, radio, newspaper, novels, billboards, bumperstickers, magazines, books, etc.

16. Summarize the need, blessings, and rewards of proper thinking.

Suggested Assignments

1. Memorize Proverbs 23:7 (KJV); Romans 12:2.
2. Memorize the five rules of thinking:
   A. Man is a thinking being.
   B. Man is always thinking.
   C. Man can think only one thought at a time.
   D. Man can control his thinking by willpower.
   E. Man is the sum total of his thoughts.

Sympathy

From the pen of the apostle Peter we read this admonition: "All of you, have unity of spirit, sympathy, love of the brethren, a tender heart and a humble mind. Do not return evil for evil or reviling for reviling; but on the contrary bless, for to this you have been called, that you may obtain a blessing" (1 Peter 3:8, 9).

Sympathy is defined as the quality of sharing another's troubles; pity; tenderness; kindness.

It could also be said that sympathy is "a suffering with" another in their troubles. It grows out of a sort of mental and spiritual acceptance of another's suffering causing an urgent desire to relieve the misery of the sufferer. Thus, although sympathy might be defined as kindness, it is actually a forerunner of this virtue, being the feeling which motivates the expression of kindness.

It is impossible truly to sympathize to the fullest extent unless we have suffered in a way similar to the suffering of the injured one. For example, if we have not lost an arm we cannot fully sympathize with one who has; we can only pity him or feel sorry for him through imagining his injury and its affect upon his life. Therefore, sympathy is a virtue that should grow stronger in us with each passing year of experiences. It is up to each of us to see that compassion does grow in us and become a part of our character.

God's Word is filled with exhortations to his people to have compassion for others. James wrote, "Religion that is pure and undefiled before God and the Father is this: to visit orphans and widows in their affliction, and to keep oneself unstained from the world" (James 1:27). God would have us feel sympathetic toward the bereaved and needy about us, and to help them. We know this is what is meant by

79

"visit orphans and widows in their affliction" because James also wrote, "If a brother or sister is ill-clad and in lack of daily food, and one of you says to them, 'Go in peace, be warmed and filled,' without giving them the things needed for the body, what does it profit?" (James 2:15, 16).

The apostle Paul wrote the Galatians to "bear one another's burdens, and so fulfill the law of Christ" (Galatians 6:2). If we have a feeling of compassion for others we will want to help them with their burdens, and it will be easy for us to fulfill the law of Christ in this. And in Romans 12:15 Paul wrote, "Rejoice with those who rejoice, weep with those who weep."

A certain lawyer, trying to test Jesus, asked who was his neighbor, since the law of Moses commanded that he love his neighbor as himself. In reply Jesus told the parable of "the good Samaritan" and when the lawyer said the injured man's neighbor was the one who had shown mercy on him, Jesus admonished him to go and do likewise.

God has always desired that man have mercy and sympathy for his fellowman. Let us cultivate this virtue and we will grow in the love of God and our associates. Each of us is capable of being touched with a feeling of compassion or pity for those in distress, even though we might lack the ability to completely sympathize by reason of a lack of experience. Ouida, British novelist of the past century, said, "There is a chord in every heart that has a sigh in it if touched aright."

Fill in Scriptures

1. _____If one member suffers, all suffer together.

2. _____Rejoice with those who rejoice, weep with those who weep.

3. _____We wailed and you did not weep.

4. _____He who closes his ear to the cry of the poor will himself cry out and not be heard.

5. _____Now when Job's three friends heard of all this evil that had come upon him, they came . . . and when they saw him . . . they raised their voices and wept. They sat with him on the ground seven days and seven nights and no one spoke a word to him, for they saw that his suffering was very great.

6. _____Be kind to one another, tenderhearted, forgiving one another, as God in Christ forgave you.

7. _____For we have not a high priest who is unable to sympathize with our weaknesses.

8. _____To the weak I became weak, that I might win the weak. I have become all things to all men, that I might by all means save some.

9. _____But now, if thou wilt forgive their sin—and if not, blot me, I pray thee out of thy book which thou hast written.

10. _____And Zacchaeus stood and said to the Lord, "Behold Lord, the half of my goods I give to the poor."

11. _____But if any one has the world's goods and sees his brother in need, yet closes his heart against him, how does God's love abide in him?

12. _____And when he drew near and saw the city he wept over it.

13. _____As a father pities his children, so the Lord pities those who fear him.

1 Corinthians 12:26   Luke 7:32   Job 2:11-13
Hebrews 4:15   Exodus 32:32   Ephesians 4:32
Proverbs 21:13   Romans 12:15   1 Corinthians 9:22
Luke 19:8   Luke 19:41   Psalms 103:13
                      1 John 3:17

Questions for Discussion

1. Define sympathy.
2. Do you feel sympathy is one of your strong characteristics?
3. Is crying a sign of weakness?
4. Generally, where do we show the most sympathy?
5. What one act, more than any other, shows God's sympathy to man?
6. What should one do who has problems of being sensitive to the suffering of others?

7. Why should we have every reason to continue to grow in this virtue?

8. Did it cause people to love Jesus less as they saw him weep over Jerusalem and at the tomb of Lazarus?

9. What did James call pure religion?

10. What is your class or the church doing in your community to manifest its sympathy and compassion to the needy, sick, lonely, the aged, and distressed?

11. Have you ever visited a ghetto, an orphanage, widows, or the fatherless?

12. Is it possible for Christians to become callous and passed feeling?

13. What did Paul say that all members should do when just one member suffers? (see 1 Corinthians 12:26).

14. Summarize the need, blessings, and rewards of sympathy.

Suggested Assignments

1. Memorize 1 Corinthians 12:26; Romans 12:15.

2. Visit someone in the convalescent home, a widow or some needy person.

3. Write a sympathy card to a family where there has been a death. (You may use the obituary column of your local newspaper).

4. Make sentences of the following words: sympathy, pity; care; callous; compassion.

Truthfulness

King Solomon, who was noted for his wisdom, wrote: "He that speaketh truth showeth forth righteousness: but a false witness deceit. . . . The lip of truth shall be established forever: but a lying tongue is but for a moment. . . Lying lips are abomination to the Lord: but they that deal truly are his delight" (Provers 12:17, 19, 22 KJV).

Truth is defined as the quality of being according to fact; a general statement of something proved to be always the case; veracity; correctness; accuracy or exactness; righteousness; godliness or faithfulness.

Paul wrote to the Ephesians, "Speaking the truth in love, we are to grow up in every way into him who is the head, into Christ. . . Therefore, putting away falsehood, let every one speak the truth with his neighbor, for we are members one of another" (Ephesians 4:15, 25).

During his trial before Pontius Pilate, Jesus said, "I have come into the world to bear witness to the truth. Every one who is of the truth hears my voice." Upon hearing this Pilate asked, "What is truth?" It is interesting to note, however, that he apparently did not even wait for an answer. This is typical of many people of the world. They may ask, but they are not really seeking the truth. Therefore, they do not hear the "voice" of Jesus. In John 17:17 is recorded this portion of the prayer of Christ to the Father on behalf of his disciples: "Sanctify them in the truth; thy word is truth." We cannot be pleasing to God if we are untruthful. His Word, the Bible, is filled with wonderful promises to those who speak and love truthfully and righteously, and of warnings of punishment to the liars.

Luther Burbank, the great plan wizard, said, "We must learn that any person who will not accept what he knows to be truth, for the very love of truth alone, is very definitely undermining his mental integrity. It will be observed that the mind of such a person gradually stops growing, for being constantly hedged in and cropped here and there, it soon learns to respect artifical fences more than freedom of growth. You have not been a very close observer of such men if you have not seen them shrivel, become commonplace, mean, without influence, without friends and without the enthusiasm of youth and growth, like a tree covered with fungus, the foliage diseased, the life gone out of the heart with dry rot, and indelibly marked for destruction—dead, but not yet handed over to the undertaker."

There is beauty in truth, and if we are careful to always tell the facts, as we believe them to be, we will establish honesty of character that will make our lives beautiful to both God and man. Our associates will have faith in the things which we do and say, and will trust and respect us. This will open to us many avenues for success in life.

A person may state something as a fact and later discover it to be incorrect, but in that case he would not be a liar. Lying is a willful misrepresentation of fact. Whenever we learn that we have been wrong in something we have said, we should have the courage to admit our error and try to correct it. We would do well to remember, however, that if we will be as careful in learning the facts as possible, and thoughtful in presenting them to others, we will be spared much of the embarrassment caused by the need for correction. Remember, ignorance is not innocence!

We should resolve to practice truth always, and to build in our heart a love of truth for its own sake, and for the joy of knowing that we will be believed.

Fill in Scriptures

1. _____And with all wicked deception for those who are to perish, because they refused to love the truth and so be saved. Therefore God sends upon them a strong delusion, to make them believe what is false, so that all may be condemned who did not believe the truth.

2. _____But as for the cowardly, the faithless, the polluted. . .

and all liars, their lot shall be in the lake that burns with fire and brimstone, which is the second death.

3._____Let no man deceive himself.

4._____While evil men and imposters will go on from bad to worse, deceivers and deceived.

5._____Now the Spirit expressly says that in later times some will depart from the faith by giving heed to deceitful spirits and doctrines of demons, through the pretensions of liars whose consciences are seared.

6._____There was no deceit in his mouth.

7._____So that we may no longer be children, tossed to and fro and carried about with every wind of doctrine, by the cunning of men, by their craftiness in deceitful wiles. Rather, speaking the truth in love. . . .

8._____For such men are false apostles, deceitful workmen, disguising themselves as apostles of Christ. And no wonder, for even Satan disguises himself as an angel of light. So it is not strange if his servants also disguise themselves as servants of righteousness.

9._____And you will know the truth, and the truth will make you free.

10._____And the Lord said to me: The prophets are prophesying lies in my name; I did not send them.

11._____False prophets will arise and . . . lead astray, if possible, even the elect.

Matthew 24:24
Ephesians 4:14, 15
2 Corinthians
11:13-15
Revelation 21:8

Jeremiah 14:14
Isaiah 53:9
2 Timothy 3:13
2 Thessalonians 2:10-12

1 Timothy 4:1-2
John 8:32
1 Corinthians 3:18

Questions for Discussion

1. Define truthfulness.
2. What satanic purpose lies behind telling lies?

3. What is a sure way to guard one's self from doctrinal errors?

4. What may one try to gain by lying?

5. Name some very common religious errors that divide and destroy.

6. Why would anyone willfully tell a lie?

7. Suggest some situations where it may take much courage to stand for the truth.

8. Can it be fatal to believe a lie?

9. What does it mean to act a lie?

10. What happens to the conscience of a habitual liar?

11. How can traditions, prejudice and emotions hinder the acceptance of the truth?

12. Summarize the need, blessings and rewards of truthfulness.

Suggested Assignments

1. Memorize 2 Thessalonians 2:10-12; 1 Timothy 4:1, 2.

2. Read the entire chapter of 1 Kings 13 and report on how a young prophet met a horrible death for sincerely believing a lie.

3. Make sentences of the following words: pretenders, liars, hypocrites, distort, misleading, trickery, pervert.

Reason

We read in Acts 24:24, 25, "And after certain days, when Felix came with his wife Drusilla, which was a Jewess, he sent for Paul, and heard him concerning the faith in Christ. And as he reasoned of righteousness, temperance, and judgment to come, Felix trembled, and answered, Go thy way for this time; when I have a convenient season, I will call for thee" (KJV).

Reason is the power or faculty of understanding; to exercise the power of thinking logically or of drawing conclusions; to persuade by argument; to prove or explain by means of the intellect.

Paul reasoned with Felix concerning righteousness, temperance and judgment to come, telling him of Christ the Saviour. When Felix heard these things his reasoning ability caused him to be fearful because he had not obeyed God. Thus we see that reason is the mental ability to consider the facts and reach a conclusion.

The more we exercise our reasoning processes the better this ability will become. Correct reasoning is not easy, and because of this many people are content to accept second-hand opinions rather than to work out one of their own. They cannot take an argument and point out the fallacies it contains. This is what enables politicians to gain and retain their hold upon certain classes of people. This is the basis of much modern advertising and is an example of what can be done by a clever writer who can catch the eye of an unthinking person. A good exercise for our power of reason is to study advertisements and pick out the false reasoning presented.

There would not be all of the religious division in the world today if people would only use their God-given reasoning powers and study God's Word for themselves. Instead, however, the majority of people are content to let someone else do their thinking for them, and so are led astray by men teaching false doctrine for worldly gain.

The really great leaders of the nation in its political, social and religious life have been people who could reason. Had Columbus not taken the time to reason he could not have discovered America. Our nation could not have grown great, and we could not now be enjoying the liberty and happiness we have, if there were not men willing and able to exercise their intellects in order to solve the nation's problems. The writer Coke said, "Reason is the life of the law."

Each of us should exercise our reasoning ability so that our mind will increase its power and enable us to become happy, intelligent adults who cannot be led astray.

Fill in Scriptures

1. _____And that we may be delivered from unreasonable and wicked men; for all men have not faith.

2. _____Immediately the word was fulfilled upon Nebuchadnezzar. He was driven from among men, and ate grass like an ox, and his body was wet with the dew of heaven till his hair grew as long as eagles' feathers, and his nails were like birds' claws. At the end of the days I, Nebuchadnezzar, lifted my eyes to heaven, and my reason returned to me, and I blessed the Most High, and praised and honored him who lives for ever.

3. _____Come now, let us reason together, says the Lord.

4. _____And as he reasoned of righteousness, temperance, and judgment to come, Felix trembled.

5. _____And Paul as his manner was, went in unto them, and three sabbath days reasoned with them out of the Scripture.

6. _____Hear now my reasoning, and listen to the pleadings of my lips. Will you speak falsely for God, and speak deceitfully for him? Will you show partiality toward him, will you plead the case for God? Will it be well with you when he searches you out? Or can you deceive him, as one deceives a man?

7._____For what will it profit a man, if he gains the whole world and forfeits his life? Or what shall a man give in return for his life?

8._____He who states his case first seems right, until the other comes and examines him.

9._____You blind guides, straining out a gnat and swallowing a camel!

10._____When I was a child, I spoke like a child, I thought like a child, I reasoned like a child; when I became a man, I gave up childish ways.

11._____Woe to those who call evil good and good evil, who put darkness for light and light for darkness, who put bitter for sweet and sweet for bitter! Woe to those who are wise in their own eyes and shrewd in their own sight!

Matthew 16:26
Acts 24:25 KJV
Isaiah 5:20
2 Thessalonians 3:2 KJV

Job 13:6-9
Matthew 23:24
Daniel 4:33-34
1 Corinthians 13:11

Acts 17:2 KJV
Proverbs 18:17
Isaiah 1:18

Questions for Discussion

1. Define reason.
2. How can the lack of reason and good judgment bring about some of the saddest experiences of life?
3. How is dialogue beneficial to making wise decisions?
4. What hinders people from carefully investigating all factors to evaluate and ascertain a logical conclusion?
5. Will there ever be a single day in our life that we will not be called upon to exercise reason and good judgment?
6. How does prejudice, tradition, resentment, hearsay, opinion, anger and jealousy affect some decisions?
7. Is it better to be right or consistent?
8. Why will some make wrong decisions even though they are aware that in doing so they must push aside their own conscience, education, council of friends and all past experience?
9. What is wrong with the person who would rather argue and

fight than reason?

10. What value is a storehouse of knowledge if it is not organized in proper prospective?

11. Why do some people "major in minors"?

12. What does it mean to "strain at a gnat and swallow a camel"?

13. How can we be helped to size things up, arrange and place in proper order, value and importance?

14. What book of the Bible is called the common sense treasury?

15. Summarize the need, blessings and rewards of reason.

Suggested Assignments

1. Memorize Isaiah 1:18; Matthew 16:26.

2. Make sentences of the following words: reason, discernment, judgment, wisdom, think.

Investigation

We read in Acts 17:11, regarding the people of Beroea, "Now these Jews were more noble than those in Thessalonica, for they received the word with all eagerness, examining the sciptures daily to see if these things were so."

Investigation is defined as careful inquiry, search, or examination to discover facts. It means searching out detailed information concerning something in which we are interested, and classifying and organizing those details in order to pass correct judgment and make decisions. When undertaking a new project it is highly important that we make thorough and careful investigation; that is, we must gather all the facts concerning any enterprise in which we propose to engage.

I'm sure each of us can think of many illustrations showing why we should investigate each situation before taking action. One of the illustrations given us in the Bible is found in Luke 14:28-33: "For which of you, desiring to build a tower, does not first sit down and count the cost, whether he has enough to complete it? Otherwise, when he has laid a foundation, and is not able to finish, all who see it begin to mock him, saying, 'This man began to build, and was not able to finish.' Or what king, going to encounter another king in war, will not sit down first and take counsel whether he is able with ten thousand to meet him who comes against him with twenty thousand? And if not, while the other is yet a great way off, he sends an embassy and asks terms of peace. So therefore, whoever of you does not renounce all that he has cannot be my disciple." Here, Jesus admonished his disciples to investigate, or examine the facts, in order to determine their course of action.

The apostle John told Christians to "believe not every spirit, but try the spirits whether they are of God: because many false prophets were gone out into the world" (1 John 4:1 KJV). He warns us to investigate and judge by God's Word.

If we make a practice of investigating and learning the facts we will be able to make our lives safe, happy and good.

Fill in Scriptures

1. _____There is a way that seems right to a man, but its end is the way to death.

2. _____He who states his case first seems right, until the other comes and examines him.

3. _____Examine yourselves, to see whether you are holding to your faith.

4. _____If anyone sins, doing any of the things which the Lord has commanded not to be done, though he does not know it, yet he is guilty and shall bear his iniquity.

5. _____In vain do they worship me, teaching as doctrines the precepts of men.

6. _____Let a man examine himself.

7. _____Anyone who goes ahead and does not abide in the doctrine of Christ does not have God.

8. _____Now these Jews were more noble than those in Thessalonica, for they received the word with all eagerness, examining the scriptures daily to see if these things were so.

9. _____But even if we, or an angel from heaven, should preach to you a gospel contrary to that which we preached to you, let him be accursed.

10. _____Not every one who says to me, "Lord, Lord," shall enter the kingdom of heaven, but he who does the will of my Father who is in heaven. On that day many will say to me, "Lord, Lord, did we not prophesy in your name. . . ? then will I declare to them, "I never knew you; depart from me, you evildoers.

11. _____Beware of false prophets.

Proverbs 16:25
2 Corinthians 13:5
2 John 9
Matthew 7:21-23

Proverbs 18:17
Leviticus 5:17
Acts 17:11
Matthew 7:15

Mark 7:7
1 Corinthians 11:28
Galatians 1:8

Questions for Discussion

1. Define investigation.
2. Why should one be compelled to make a biblical examination of all doctrines taught by the church where he attends?
3. How important is it to track down the footsteps of truth in God's plan of salvation for men?
4. How can traditions, customs, opinions, hearsay and prejudice become barriers to clear observation and close examination of scriptural truths?
5. How much weight should we place in rumors?
6. Approximately one new business in 35 go on to succeed. What does this tell you about man's habits of investigation and examination?
7. Why are there hundreds of denominations with conflicting doctrines?
8. What will ultimately happen to the one who allows his friends, his conscience and his feelings to guide him?
9. Do you feel that most people are what they are religiously because of scriptural reasons or because of human reasons?
10. Have you seriously examined yourself along with God's Word in hopes of discovering just what his plan is for your life?
11. Is one's conscience a sufficient guide in matters of marriage, traveling, business or religion?
12. Summarize the needs, blessings and rewards of investigation.

Suggested Assignments

1. Memorize Proverbs 14:12; Proverbs 18:17.
2. Give Scripture for God's plan of salvation.
3. Investigate and give reasons why you believe that the church you attend is scriptural in name, doctrine and practice.

Wisdom

"If any of you lacks wisdom, let him ask God who gives to all men generously and without reproaching, and it will be given him" (James 1:5).

Wisdom is defined as the faculty of forming a sound judgment in a matter; knowledge digested by thought; discernment based on experience of men and things.

There is a difference between wisdom and knowledge in that wisdom is the ability to effectively use the knowledge, or learning, which we have acquired. Wisdom is mental balance, maturity of judgment, sobriety of thought with regard to the major problems of life. It cannot be expected that children will have wisdom in this truest and deepest sense of its meaning, but they can develop judgment, caution, discretion and a thoughtful analysis of acts and plans which will ripen into mature wisdom.

In recording the childhood of Christ, Luke wrote, "And Jesus increased in wisdom and in stature, and in favor with God and man" (Luke 2:52). It is expected that children will endeavor to develop this worthwhile characteristic, even though it be one that requires much time and effort to acquire. Abraham Lincoln said, "I don't think much of a man who is not wiser today than he was yesterday."

Since wisdom is the ability to use our learning judiciously, it follows that we must first have knowledge to use. We can then carefully consider this knowledge to determine how to use it most effectively. Our consideration will depend to a large degree upon our own experience, but probably to an even greater degree upon our observations of the experiences of others.

The Bible is filled with examples of wisdom, and of praise for the wise. James wrote, "Who is wise and understanding among you? By his good life let him show his works in the meekness of wisdom. But if you have bitter jealousy and selfish ambition in your hearts, do not boast and be false to the truth. This wisdom is not such as comes down from above, but is earthly, unspiritual, devilish. . . But the wisdom from above is first pure, then peaceable, gentle, open to reason, full of mercy and good fruits, without uncertainty or insincerity" (James 3:13-17).

Each of us should make certain that the things we do and say follow careful thought, rather than impulse, and we should pray to God for the wisdom to make the best possible judgments regarding our daily decisions, activities and problems.

Fill in Scriptures

1. _____If any of you lacks wisdom, let him ask God who gives to all men generously and without reproaching, and it will be given him.

2. _____The fear of the Lord is the beginning of knowledge; fools despise wisdom and instruction.

3. _____Every one then who hears these words of mine and does them will be like a wise man who built the house upon the rock.

4. _____Happy is the man who finds wisdom, and the man who gets understanding.

5. _____Look carefully then how you walk, not as unwise men but as wise, making the most of the time, because the days are evil.

6. _____Let your heart hold fast my words; keep my commandments and live; do not forget, and do not turn away from the words of my mouth. Get wisdom; get insight. Do not forsake her, and she will keep you; love her, and she will guard you. The beginning of wisdom is this: Get wisdom, and whatever you get, get insight. Prize her highly, and she will exalt you; she will honor you if you embrace her. She will place on your head a fair garland; she will bestow on you a beautiful crown.

7. _____Who is wise and understanding among you? By his

good life let him show his works in meekness of wisdom. But if you have bitter jealousy and selfish ambition in your hearts, do not boast and be false to the truth. This wisdom is not such as comes down from above, but is earthly, unspiritual, devilish.

8. _____Fools, when will you be wise? He who planted the ear, does he not hear? He who formed the eye, does he not see?

9. _____Better is a poor and wise youth than an old and foolish king, who will no longer take advice.

10. _____Be wise as serpents and inocent as doves.

Matthew 7:24	Proverbs 1:7	James 1:5
Matthew 10:16	Ecclesiastes 4:13	Psalms 94:8-9
James 3:13-15	Ephesians 5:15-16	Proverbs 3:13
	Proverbs 4:4-9	

Questions for Discussion

1. Define wisdom.

2. What assurance have we that God will give us wisdom?

3. What is the difference between wisdom and knowledge?

4. Name some vocations or activities that require a special amount of wisdom.

5. What will happen to a church that fails to develop wise leadership?

6. Do you feel that you are developing insight and perception to the basic priorities of life?

7. Are you developing a basic knowledge of God's will with a desire to make proper use of it?

8. Are you making progress in learning to deal with the important facts that especially relate to the good life?

9. Are you studious, disciplined, prayerful, discerning and a good listener?

10. Name some prerequisites to making wise decisions?

11. In what situation is wisdom needed the most?

12. Can you name some foolish decisions and their end-results?

13. Name several ways that wisdom can be developed within an individual.

14. Summarize the need, blessings and rewards of wisdom.

Suggested Assignments

1. Memorize James 1:5; Ecclesiastes 4:13.

2. Make sentences with the following words: foolish, wise, heedless, dull, stupid, foolish.

3. Jesus said, "The children of the world are wiser than the children of light." List some possible ways the church might exercise more wisdom.

Punctuality

"To every thing there is a season, and a time to every purpose under the heaven: a time to be born, and a time to die; a time to plant, and a time to pluck up that which is planted; a time to kill, and a time to heal; a time to break down, and a time to build up; a time to weep, and a time to laugh; a time to mourn, and a time to dance; a time to cast away stones, and a time to gather stones together; a time to embrace, and a time to refrain from embracing; a time to get, and a time to lose; a time to keep, and a time to cast away; a time to rend, and a time to sew; a time to keep silence, and a time to speak; a time to love, and a time to hate; a time of war, and a time of peace" (Ecclesiastes 3:1-8 KJV).

Punctuality is the quality of being prompt, especially in keeping an appointment or engagement; of observing, or doing, at the precise and exact time.

Some people can be depended upon to do whatever they are supposed to do at the time they are supposed to do it, and the same people are seldom late for an appointment because they realize the value of time. Others, to whom time appears to be of little value, are almost always late. They seem to be in a constant rush and complain of a lack of time. The fact is, everyone has been given exactly the same amount of hours, minutes, and seconds in each day. Are those who complain of a need for more time actually busier than others? Of course, such could be the case, but in most instances their trouble lies in a lack of respect for time, and they have acquired the habit of "putting off."

The apostle Paul told the Colossians to "Conduct yourselves wisely toward outsiders, making the most of the time" (Colossians 4:5).

And to the Galatians he wrote, "Let us not grow weary in well-doing, for in due season we shall reap, if we do not lose heart" (Galatians 6:9). God's Word is filled with exhortations to respect time and use it well.

Punctuality is really a matter of habit—one that each and every one of us can acquire. If we could only realize how valuable this gift of time is, how very many things we have to do, and how God would have us use our time to work in his kingdom, we would all strive to acquire the habit of punctuality. No Christian should ever be careless of so great a blessing! Even the great in the eyes of the world realize the value of punctuality. As an example, Lord Nelson, one of England's greatest naval officers, said, "I owe all my success in life to having been always a quarter of an hour beforehand." We may be sure that punctuality is the habit of ALL who attain success.

To make this one of our own characteristics it might be well for each of us to "take stock" of our life and see if we "make the most of our time." If we will regulate our hours to do our work first and then have the leftover time for our own, we may be surprised to find that our work can be done promptly and the time belonging to us will become more pleasant than it is when we try to take our leisure first and delay our work.

Fill in Scriptures

1. _____ Look carefully then how you walk, not as unwise men but as wise, making the most of the time.

2. _____ For everything there is a season and a time for every matter under heaven.

3. _____ Now Peter and John were going up to the temple at the hour of prayer, the ninth hour.

4. _____ At the appointed time I will return to you.

5. _____ In the morning Jonathan went out into the field to the appointment with David.

6. _____ So the Lord sent a pestilence upon Israel from the morning until the appointed time; and there died of the people from Dan to Beer-sheba seventy thousand men.

7. _____ In his days Hiel of Bethel built Jericho; he laid its foundation at the cost of Abiram his first born, and

set up its gates at the cost of his youngest son Segub, according to the word of the Lord, which he spoke by Joshua the son of Nun. (God kept this appointment with death even as he had promised 400 years previous —Joshua 6:26).

8 _____ "How long will you be gone, and when will you return?" So it pleased the king to send me; and I set him a time.

9._____ Thou wilt arise and have pity on Zion; it is time to favor her; the appointed time has come.

10._____ So Amasa went to summon Judah; but he delayed beyond the set time which had been appointed him.

11._____ Even the stork in the heavens knows her times; and the turtledove, swallow, and crane keep the time of their coming; but my people know not the ordinance of the Lord.

12._____ The bridegroom came, and those who were ready went in with him to the marriage feast; and the door was shut. Afterward the other maidens came also, saying, "Lord, Lord, open to us." But he replied, "Truly, I say to you, I do not know you."

Ephesians 5:15	Genesis 18:14	Ecclesiastes 3:1
Acts 3:1	1 Kings 16:34	1 Samuel 20:35
2 Samuel 24:15	Nehemiah 2:6	Psalms 102:13
Jeremiah 8:7	2 Samuel 20:5	Matthew 25:10-12

Questions for Discussion

1. Define punctuality.

2. What ultimately will happen to the person who is habitually late for work or other engagements?

3. What would happen to the great transportation system in this country if men would disregard time and schedules? Would not our country be in utter chaos?

4. It is proper to say that "appointments once made, become debts"?

5. Explain how we waste the time of others when we are lacking in punctuality.

6. Can one be successful or even be respected that has little concern for time, schedules or punctuality?

7. What attitude does business have toward the individual who does not pay his bills on time?

8. Shakespeare said, "Better be three hours too soon than one minute too late." Why should he make such a statement?

9. "Better late than never" is not half as good a maxim as "better never late." Do you agree?

10. When George Washington's secretary was late he excused himself by saying that his watch was slow. The President replied, "You must get a new watch, or I must get a new secretary." Do you feel the president was too harsh?

11. How does the latecomer to Bible class or worship services hinder?

12. Summarize the need, blessings and rewards of punctuality.

Suggested Assignments

1. Memorize Ephesians 5:15, 16; Matthew 25:10-12.

2. Make sentences with the following words: punctuality, time, exact, appointments, schedule.

3. Make an estimate of how many millions of people each week are discouraged, disappointed, or angry because of late or broken appointments. Consider employers, Bible teachers, preachers, husbands and wives, dates while courting, transportation systems, doctor's appointment, etc.

Courtesy

Peter wrote, "All of you have unity of spirit, sympathy, love of the brethren, a tender heart and a humble mind. Do not return evil for evil or reviling for reviling; but on the contrary bless. . ." (1 Peter 3:8, 9).

Courtesy is politeness combined with kindness; it is consideration for the feelings of others.

We should train ourselves to have consideration for other people, and to speak and act kindly toward them. The importance of courteous behavior cannot be overestimated. Along with kindness and tact, it is one of the fine things of life, and will do much to increase the usefulness of the individual to his family and to the social group at large. A courteous consideration for the rights and opinions of others will be a powerful factor in making a person acceptable and respected by his associates.

When we are kind and pleasant we are behaving courteously, and people are happy to be our friends, and they will enjoy being with us. It is a very valuable thing to be able to make, and keep, friends, and courtesy helps us in this more than almost anything else. Those who are courteous avoid many of the combative encounters which cause ill-feeling and often lead to the loss of friends. When we become cross and of an ugly spirit, we forget to be courteous.

We've often heard it said, "Practice makes perfect." Let us practice courtesy every day and it will, in time, become a wonderful part of our lives.

It takes a kindly spirit to be courteous. Some are able, it seems, to shock others by their ill manners. To behave oneself in a rude manner will always be unseemly. There is never a place for discourtesy. We should always be careful not to offend others. Courteous conduct is always attractive and pleasing to all.

Manners give the measure of a man. "Do not return evil for evil or reviling for reviling but on the contrary bless" (1 Peter 3:9). Some are rude in their manner of speaking, driving an automobile, waiting in lines or pushing their way through a crowd. Others show their lack of courtesy by throwing loose paper and coke cans on people's lawns and on streets, or dropping gum on sidewalks. Rudeness is manifested in seeking out the best or most comfortable chair in the presence of others and wanting to be served first. When one throws his clothes carelessly around or furniture or blasts the radio and TV so loudly that it disturbs others, he is rude. We must not disregard the needs, rights and comforts of others. Butting in on someone else's conversation can be very discourteous. There are a thousand ways to show courtesy or the lack of it.

Fill in Scriptures

1. _____Pay all of them their dues . . . respect to whom respect is due, honor to whom honor is due.

2. _____ I preferred to do nothing without your consent in order that your goodness might not be by compulsion but of your own free will.

3. _____When a stranger sojourns with you in your land, you shall not do him wrong. The stranger who sojourns with you shall be to you as the native among you, and you shall love him as yourself.

4. _____Claudius Lysias to his Excellency the governor Felix, greetings.

5. _____Honor all men. Love the brotherhood. Fear God. Honor the emperor.

6. _____Love is not . . . arrogant or rude.

7. _____Grace to you and peace from God the Father and our Lord Jesus Christ.

8. _____For if a man with gold rings and in fine clothing comes into your assembly, and a poor man in shabby clothing also comes in, and you pay attention to the one who

wears the fine clothing and say, "Have a seat here, please," while you say to the poor man, "Stand here," or, "Sit at my feet," have you not made distinctions among yourselves, and become judges with evil thoughts?

9._____Outdo one another in showing honor.

10._____We were gentle among you . . . because you had become very dear to us.

11._____To the saints and faithful brethren in Christ at Colossae: Grace of you and peace from God our Father. We always thank God, the Father of our Lord Jesus Christ, when we pray for you, because we have heard of your faith.

James 2:2-4	Galatians 1:3	Philemon 14
1 Corinthians 13:5	Acts 23:26	1 Thessalonians 2:7,8
Romans 12:10	1 Peter 2:17	Leviticus 19:33-34
Romans 13:7	Colossians 1:2-3	

Questions for Discussion

1. Define courtesy.
2. Explain how courtesy, polished manners, even gallantry can be a great blessing to mankind.
3. Could we learn courtesy from an airline stewardess or a waitress in the restuarant?
4. Why does courtesy sometime become neglected in the home?
5. Should Christians be less courtesous than the receptionist in the doctor's office, or the clerk in the grocery store?
6. How can we increase courtesy in the church, especially on being gracious to visitors?
7. Are you an attentive listener?
8. Do you interrupt while others are talking?
9. Explain how courtesy is sometimes forgotten while driving a car, walking along the sidewalk, standing in line, and communicating with others.
10. Whose responsibility is it to be courteous in the church?
11. Summarize the need, blessings and rewards of being courteous.

Suggested Assignment

1. Memorize Romans 13:7; Romans 12:10.

2. Make sentences with the following words: courtesy, good manners, gallantry, respect, honor, rude, offensive, aloof.

3. Go out of your way to speak to someone at school or at church services that you don't know. Be cordial, friendly and interested in them. Report your new experience.

4. Commend or show appreciation to someone whom you respect or appreciate for untiring services and helpfulness.

Unselfishness

"Do nothing from selfishness or conceit, but in humility count others better than yourselves. Let each of you look not only to his own interests, but also to the interests of others" (Philippians 2:3, 4).

Unselfishness might be defined as having no thought for one's self; putting the wishes and advantages of others before one's own; consideration for the comfort, happiness, or rights of others.

This is not a negative virtue indicating merely the absence of a selfish disposition. It is altogether positive in character and denotes a disposition to share what one has with another, or with others. This means sharing opportunity for advancement, sharing personal possessions, sharing joys and pleasures, and giving to others any or all of the good things one may have.

Unselfishness brings a real joy. It is a pleasure to give another the better seat, the "biggest piece" of pie, or the more promising advantage in a competitive enterprise. This is not a natural virtue but one that must be cultivated with real effort.

The great apostle Paul told the Ephesian brethren, "In all things I have shown you that by so toiling one must help the weak, remembering the words of the Lord Jesus, how he said, 'It is more blessed to give than to receive' " (Acts 20:35). Jesus established this principle both by word and by example, and it was taught and practiced by the apostles. It is just as true today as it was in the days of the apostles.

If we are to be obedient and pleasing to God we must acquire an unselfish disposition and help those about us. Since it is a difficult virtue to obtain, we should begin at once to practice the acts of kindness and thoughtfulness which mark the unselfish attitude.

Fill in Scriptures

1. _____We who are strong ought to bear with the failings of the weak, and not to please ourselves.

2. _____He must increase, but I must decrease.

3. _____Bear one another's burdens, and so fulfill the law of Christ.

4. _____If any man would come after me, let him deny himself and take up his cross and follow me.

5. _____Be subject to one another out of reverence for Christ.

6. _____But whatever gain I had, I counted as loss for the sake of Christ.

7. _____If he has wronged you at all, or owes you anything, charge that to my account.

8. _____Just as I try to please all men in everything I do, not seeking my own advantage.

9. _____Their extreme poverty have overflowed in a wealth of liberality on their part. For they gave according to their means, of their own free-will, begging us earnestly for the favor of taking part in the relief of the saints—and this, not as we expected, but first they gave themselves to the Lord and to us by the will of God.

10. _____And Zacchaeus stood and said to the Lord, "Behold, Lord, the half of my goods I give to the poor; and if I have defrauded anyone of anything, I restore it fourfold."

11. _____Do nothing from selfishness or conceit, but in humility count others better than yourselves. Let each of you look not only to his own interests, but also to the interests of others.

12. _____But I do not account my life of any value nor as precious to myself, if only I may accomplish my course.

13. _____For you know the grace of our Lord Jesus Christ, that though he was rich, yet for your sake he became poor, so that by his poverty you might become rich.

Galatians 6:2   Ephesians 5:21   Matthew 16:24
Philemon 18   2 Corinthians 8:9   Acts 20:24
Romans 15:1   Philippians 2:3   Luke 19:8
John 3:30   2 Corinthians 8:2-5   1 Corinthians 10:33
                             Philippians 3:7

Questions for Discussion

1. Define unselfishness.

2. What is the normal reaction one has to the person who is excessively concerned with himself?

3. How does a person develop a gracious spirit of liberality?

4. Is selfishness always readily detected in a person?

5. Is it true that only an unselfish person can become totally involved in church activities such as teaching and saving souls?

6. Can there be any hope in the world to come for the person who has an exclusive regard for his own comforts, interests and advantages?

7. Why are men selfish when joy and inward peace come by surrendering themselves and looking to the interest and needs of others?

8. How do you respond to a warm and generous, unselfish attitude?

9. Must all men put forth special effort to overcome selfishness?

10. In what circumstances are we most apt to be tempted to selfishness?

11. Summarize the need, blessings and rewards of unselfishness.

Suggested Assignments

1. Memorize Matthew 16:24; Philippians 2:3.

2. Make sentences with the following words: unselfishness, generous, selfish, self-love.

3. Do a good deed this week anonymously.

Spirituality

To the Romans Paul wrote, "Those who live according to the flesh set their minds on the things of the flesh, but those who live according to the Spirit set their minds on the things of the Spirit. To set the mind on the flesh is death, but to set the mind on the Spirit is life and peace" (Romans 8:5, 6).

Spirituality may be defined as the state or quality of being neither physical nor material; soul as apart from matter; unworldliness; elevation of mind.

Spirituality is contrasted with materiality. One whose thoughts and affections are bound up with things material is not usually regarded as being spiritually minded. The more spiritually minded man becomes, the more he is like God, Paul said. "I appeal to you therefore, brethren, by the mercies of God, to present your bodies as a living sacrifice, holy and acceptable to God, which is your spiritual worship. Do not be conformed to this world but be transformed by the renewal of your mind, that you may prove what is the will of God, what is good and acceptable and perfect" (Romans 12:1, 2).

And to Titus he wrote, "For the grace of God has appeared for the salvation of all men, training us to renounce irreligion and worldly passions, and to live sober, upright, and godly lives in this world" (Titus 2:11, 12).

Like everything else, spirituality grows by means of what it feeds upon. "God is Spirit, and those who worship him must worship in spirit and truth" (John 4:24). Jesus said, ". . .thy world is truth" (John 17:17). If we would grow in spirituality, we must feed on God's Word.

Today one may witness the latest craze or fad in strange styles of

111

worship. Many think that religion has "gone bananas," and so it has in many places. This is really nothing new to the Bible. Seeking a wild experience in religion can actually be accomplished, "because they refused to love the truth . . . God sends upon them a strong delusion, to make them believe, what is false" (2 Thessalonians 2:10-11 RSV).

Much of this recent strange movement began with the "Flower Generation," that copped out with drugs and violence. Their leaders are often self-appointed "reverends," many of whom attempt to brainwash their followers. No one dare deny that they receive their kicks, for God had long ago announced that they receive a "strong delusion." No doubt many of them do take off on their round trip to Nirvana. Wild bursts of growth develop among those who are little acquainted in Scripture. Most of it is just an emotional jag—attempts to receive self-centered blessing through the ecstatic experience of escape. True followers will have no part nor lot in such cheapness of religion.

Fill in Scriptures

1. _____Have this mind among yourselves, which you have in Christ Jesus, who though he was in the form of God, did not count equality with God, a thing to be grasped, but emptied himself, taking the form of a servant.

2. _____But we have the mind of Christ.

3. _____If anyone thinks that he is a prophet, or spiritual, he should acknowledge that what I am writing to you is a command of the Lord.

4. _____And so, from the day we heard of it, we have not ceased to pray for you, asking that you may be filled with the knowledge of his will in all spiritual wisdom and understanding, to lead a life worthy of the Lord, fully pleasing to him, bearing fruit in every good work and increasing in the knowledge of God.

5. _____I have been crucified with Christ; it is no longer I who live, but Christ who lives in me.

6. _____And like living stones be yourselves built into a spiritual house, to be a holy priesthood, to offer spiritual sacrifices.

7. _____God is spirit, and those who worship him must worship in spirit and truth.

8._____To set the mind on the flesh in death, but to set the mind on the Spirit is life and peace. For the mind that is set on the flesh is hostile to God; it does not submit to God's law, indeed it cannot; and those who are in the flesh cannot please God. But you are not in the flesh, you are in the Spirit, if in fact the Spirit of God really dwells in you. Any one who does not have the Spirit of Christ does not belong to him.

9._____But the natural man receiveth not the things of the Spirit of God: for they are foolishness unto him: neither can he know them, because they are spiritually discerned.

10._____But the fruit of the Spirit is love, joy, patience, peace, kindness, goodness, faithfulness, gentleness, self-control.

11._____And I, brethren, could not speak unto you as unto spiritual, but as unto carnal, even as unto babes in Christ. I have fed you with milk, and not with meat; for hitherto ye were not able to bear it, neither yet now are ye able. For ye are yet carnal: for whereas there is among you envying, and strife, and divisions, are ye not carnal, and walk as men?

Galatians 5:22	1 Corinthians 2:16	Philippians 2:5-7
1 Corinthians 14:37	Colossians 1:9	1 Peter 2:5
John 4:24	Romans 8:6-9	1 Corinthians 2:14 KJV
1 Corinthians 3:1-3 KJV	Galatians 2:20	

COMMENT: Some think that real spirituality is climbing into some high emotional peak, or "flying on cloud nine." Indeed, Christ causes us to be emotionally high; however, there is much more to it than looking for "spiritual kicks." Whoopee religion will always come and go. Spirituality is shown in our attitudes toward God, man and everyday routine affairs. It is doing an honest day's work, keeping house, being a good neighbor. We admit that spirituality is a silent inner glow that radiates, but again it reaches far beyond that. It is developing continually and gradually in Christian character and service that glorifies Christ. Pure religion is visiting those in need and keeping one's self unspotted from the world. A more valid test of spirituality is shown in one's concern in benevolence, teaching, witnessing, living with right attitudes, rendering a complete Christian service, and meekly facing the many trials that come our way. It is not so much the feeling one gets out of it but rather what he puts into it. What does God get out of it?

Questions for Discussion

1. Define spirituality.
2. What one person helped you the most to be spiritual?
3. Define and explain how the following affect spirituality: flesh, world, Satan.
4. Is it possible to maintain a steady spiritual level without highs and lows?
5. How do friends and associates affect our spiritual level?
6. Define each of the following: natural man, carnal man, spiritual man.
7. Which of the following seems to help you the most to closer relationship with Christ: personal Bible study, the worship assemblies, teaching someone God's will, prayer or just being around spirtual people?
8. Summarize the need and blessings of spirituality.

Assignments

1. Memorize Philippians 2:16; John 4:24.
2. Make sentences with the following words: spiritual, carnal, fleshly, devout.
3. Take notes on the preacher's sermon.

Using Weaknesses in Character as Stepping-Stones to Greatness

Every person has his weak spots in character. It is most important that we be aware of them and face them lest they lead to our defeat. We can actually defeat and make our weaknesses become our assets. Even as Paul said, "When I am weak I am strong." Each person can use his weak points as stepping stones to victory. Character training takes deep interest in what a person lacks. We must all search our hearts for our predominant failing—then learn how to fight against it. Our very first need is then to discover what is worst in us. This is just as important as discovering what is best in us. This can be done in these series of studies. It is vital that we know clearly those weaknesses of character to which we are most frequently tempted.

It is wrong to believe that because we are tempted that we are wicked. James tells us "blessed is the one who endures trial for when he has stood the test he will receive the crown of life" (James 1:12). The blessing is two-fold: it reveals our weak spots in character and gives us opportunity for gaining merit by refusing to surrender to it. Through examination these studies will help reveal our basic defect. Our predominant fault must be dealt with else it will prevail. Some persons are inclined principally to laziness, others to sensuality, anger or materialism, etc. The predominant weak spot may remain hidden to the one possessing it without some kind of training. Weakness in character can be uncovered, brought out in the open and done battle with. No real progress can be made until the master fault is dug up by examination and brought to light.

The secret of character training is to strengthen the weak spots. They must be identified and called by their right and ugly names. The predominate fault will always seek to be covered up in its hiding place to prevent being recognized. "Sometimes the master sin can be detected by discovering what defect makes us most angry when we are accused of it."

Moses used his weakness of character as stepping stones to greatness. "Now the man Moses was very meek" (Numbers 12:3). This was not always his true nature, in fact the very opposite. It was, no doubt, developed through self-examination in character study. He was at one time probably very "hot headed." He killed an Egyptian, in a fit of anger smashed "the tables of stone," and in uncontrolled anger "smote the rock." Here is a man who turned the worst in himself into the best. He became exceedingly meek. Moses fortified the breaches of his soul. They became his strongest points. The Bible is filled with many great saints who have become the very opposite of what they once were.

Let us make the area in life in which we are prone to be defeated the area of our greatest victory. People will say then, I knew him when . . . all to the glory of God.

In dealing with self there are times when we must look for the worst. In dealing with others we must look for the best. Trying to achieve this with prayer, singleness of purpose and study will bring victory.